Inspirationals, Quotes and Sayings

Lady Kimberly Motes Doty

ASIN: BOC3S51J55 Kindle

ISBN-13: 979-8-39379-303-6 Paperback Amazon

ASIN: BOC47YKSYG

ISBN-13: 979-8-39482-421-0 Hardcover Amazon

ASIN: BOC5BQ7C3D

ISBN: 978-1-0882-4858-4 Paperback

Dedication

In the realm of inspiration, where wisdom and beauty intertwine, we embark on a journey dedicated to Love and to God. This sacred voyage is for all those who hold Love dear, those who seek its embrace, those who mend their wounded hearts, and those who revel in its divine embrace.

To Love, the eternal force that binds us all, this book is devoted. It is a testament to the power of Love, a beacon for souls yearning to bask in its radiant glow. For Love is the essence that ignites our spirits, the elixir that fuels our existence. It is a force that knows no boundaries, transcending time and space, weaving its magic into the very fabric of our lives.

And to God, the grand architect of Love, we offer our heartfelt gratitude. For in His infinite wisdom, He bestowed upon us the greatest commandment of all: to Love. As Matthew 22:37-40 and Mark 12:30-31 proclaim, there is no higher calling than to love the Lord with all our heart, soul, and mind, and to extend that love to our fellow beings.

Let this book be a sanctuary of inspiration, a sanctuary where Love and God converge. May its pages ignite the flame of love within your soul, reminding you of the boundless capacity to love and be loved. May it serve as a guiding light, leading you towards the path of compassion, kindness, and empathy. And may it remind you that, in the realm of Love, miracles manifest, hearts heal, and dreams take flight.

To Love and to God, we dedicate this collection of inspirations, quotes, and sayings. May it be a testament to the extraordinary power and transformative nature of Love. May it awaken your spirit, uplift your soul, and instill within you a profound sense of purpose and connection. Embrace the wisdom within these pages, for they are the whispers of Love and the echoes of God's eternal grace.

With love and reverence, we embark on this journey together. Let the words within this book be your guiding light, leading you to a life filled with love, joy, and divine inspiration.

Acknowledgment

In the realm of boundless inspiration, I humbly acknowledge the divine presence of God, for without His unwavering love, the pages of this book "Inspirationals, Quotes and Sayings" would remain blank, devoid of purpose and meaning.

In the depths of my heart, I am eternally grateful to God for bestowing upon me the vision to perceive the profound beauty and enchantment that resides within the tapestry of everyday life. It is through His grace that I am able to grasp the extraordinary in the ordinary and draw inspiration from the simplest of moments.

With each word penned on these pages, I am reminded that it is not the circumstances we find ourselves in that define us, but rather the choices we make and the perspective we embrace. It is our attitude, our unwavering belief in the power of positivity, that shapes our reality.

This is part of why this is my motto:

"Everyday is your day for your happily ever after. What are you doing today to make it happen?"

In the presence of God's divine love and guidance, may this collection of inspirationals, quotes, and sayings ignite a flame within your soul, empowering you to embrace each moment with unwavering faith and boundless joy.

To my incredible family and friends,

I am profoundly grateful for your unwavering support and belief in my creative journey. Without your love, encouragement, and willingness to share your own experiences, this book, "Inspirationals, Quotes and Sayings," would not have been possible.

Each of you has played an integral role in shaping the pages of this book. Your stories, triumphs, and even your struggles have served as a wellspring of inspiration for me. Through your resilience, determination, and unwavering spirit, you have shown me the true power of the human heart.

Life is not always a picturesque path strewn with roses. It can be riddled with challenges, heartbreak, and uncertainty. Yet, in the face of adversity, you have taught me how to embrace a different perspective, a more uplifting approach. You have shown me that even in the darkest of times, we can find a glimmer of light.

As I penned these words, I was reminded of the incredible strength within each of you. Your unwavering faith in the beauty of life has inspired me to dream out loud. Together, we have created an inspirational roadmap, illuminating the way towards a brighter future.

To my family, thank you for being the pillars of strength in my life.

Your love and support have lifted me up when I needed it most. Your unwavering belief in my abilities has given me the courage to leap into the unknown. You are the lights of my life and I would be lost without you.

To my friends, thank you for your constant presence and

unwavering friendship. Your laughter, shared adventures, and heartfelt conversations have fueled my creativity and enriched my soul. You have shown me the true meaning of unconditional love and support. You are my soul sisters and my soul friends and I adore you so!

I am eternally grateful for each and every one of you. Your presence in my life has enriched it beyond measure. May the words within these pages serve as a reminder of the incredible power we possess to shape our lives, to embrace the beauty that lies within, and to create our own unique tapestry of inspiration.

Sometimes by simply dreaming out loud about how we want our lives to be, we are creating an inspirational plan to make our lives better - our lives, our love our way.

With boundless gratitude,

~ Lady Kimberly

Everyday is your chance for
your happily ever after.
What are you doing today to
make yours happen?
~ Lady Kimberly

CONTENTS

Page Blank Intentionally

Preface

It isn't very often in life we are faced with our own mortality and live beyond that point in our lives to be able to talk about it, let alone write about it, however I have been blessed enough to do so. This book is a culmination of a some of the things I believe about God, love, life and living.

At the end of 2019, just a day before Thanksgiving, I was given the news that I had cancer. Some thanksgiving gift, right? To make this even more devastating, my youngest daughter and most of her family were stricken with this really serious flu-like illness over the Christmas and New Year's break. We found out later that it was COVID. Shortly afterwards, the whole world found out and we all found ourselves in a lockdown for a few months. As the world was going into the COVID lockdown, I was coming out of a long surgery to remove the cancer and beginning my long recovery from cancer.

One of the first thing to happen when you have to tell the people you love that you have cancer, especially when you have lost both parents to cancer, is so much guilt. How did I let this happen? How could I have let me family down so terribly? How did I miss the signs especially when I practice natural health? It's completely overwhelming.

The next thing to happen is reevaluating every aspect of your life from what you believe to every missed opportunity, to knowing you will never live a life you consider ordinary again. Suddenly every day becomes a precious gift. You look for and find the magic in everyday life. Everyday life will never again be ordinary for you. Living a life full of passion, full of love, full of life becomes your priority.

I found I really wanted to BE the example for my family, not just tell them about what I believed about things, what was precious to me and what was, well BS to me. It all seemed important.

Yes, having cancer changes you.

Having cancer twice really, truly, changes you.

I will never be the person I was before cancer and before the pandemic.

And that's ok.

That person was just waiting to die anyway.

This person, this woman, she's living each and every day full of passion, full of love and full of life. She sees the magic in the sunrise, feels the beauty in all the colors of the rainbow found in the colors of the clam shell angel wings on the beach, hears all the whispers of the angels in the pure white feathers floating on the breeze and in the surf and lying in the sand, experiences all the magic and beauty found in the plain brown pin shells as they are opened up into perfect hearts on the beach, and her soul soars in the love affair she found when she fell in love with God with her all her heart and with all her soul and with all her mind and with all her strength the first time and each and every time again and again like all perfect passionate love affairs happen that are everlasting and forever.

This woman, she is finally living her happily ever after.

~ Lady Kimberly

Biblical Inspirations

THE 1ST AND GREATEST COMMANDMENT

Do you know the First and
Great commandment & the
Second from the Bible?

THE FIRST & GREATEST COMMANDMENT

"Thou shalt love the Lord thy God with all thy heart, and with all thy soul, and with all thy mind. This is the First and Greatest commandment."
Matthew 22:37-38

AND THE SECOND COMMANDMENT

"And the second is like it:
'Love your neighbor as
yourself.'"
Matthew 22:39

FALLING IN LOVE WITH GOD

Falling in love with God with all of your heart, with all of your soul and with all of your mind.

This is what Matthew 22:37-38 is telling us is the First and greatest commandment.

Falling in love is that all encompassing, nothing can ever tear my love away from you. I am addicted to your love, I can't get enough of you, I can't wait to be with you, I can't wait to see you, you touch every part of my heart and soul and I will never do anything to betray you kind of love.

Are you in love with God this way, with all your hear, all your soul and all your mind?

LOVING GOD WITH ALL THY HEART, SOUL, AND MIND

"Thou shalt love the
Lord God with all thy
heart, and all thy soul,
and with all thy mind.
This is the First and
Greatest commandment.
And the second is like
unto it: 'Thou shalt love
thy neighbor as thyself.'"
Matthew 22:37-39
~ Lady Kimberly

LOVING EVERYONE AS YOU LOVE YOURSELF

Do you love every person you meet as much as you love yourself?
That rude person on the phone call?
That even more obnoxious person that cut you off in traffic making you slam on your brakes and spill your $12 drink all over your shirt and car?
How about that person that yelled at you because they were having a really bad day and you just happened to be there?
Matthew 22:39 days we are to love each of them as much as we love ourselves.
Did you ask God to bless and help any of them have a better day or just let it make your day feel worse?

ALL LIFE BEGINS AS A CLEAN SLATE

Its up to us to make it good, bad, or otherwise.

We are given life.
All begins as a
It's up to us to
make it good, bad
or otherwise.
Genesis 2:7 "Then the Lord God formed the man of dust from the ground and breathed into his nostrils the breath of life."
~ Lady Kimberly

PERFECT LOVE CASTS OUT FEAR

Perfect Love Casts Out Fear

1 John 14:18 "There is no fear in love, but perfect love casts out fear. For fear has to do with punishing and all fear is cast out."

When someone truly, genuinely loves you, their love carries no fear with it. You do not have to be afraid of their love. Their love will be like the creator's love, it will "cast out fear" and love you just as you are.

If you are afraid to love someone or keep having doubts, it may be the Holy Spirit warning you this situation isn't right for you.

Lady Kimberly

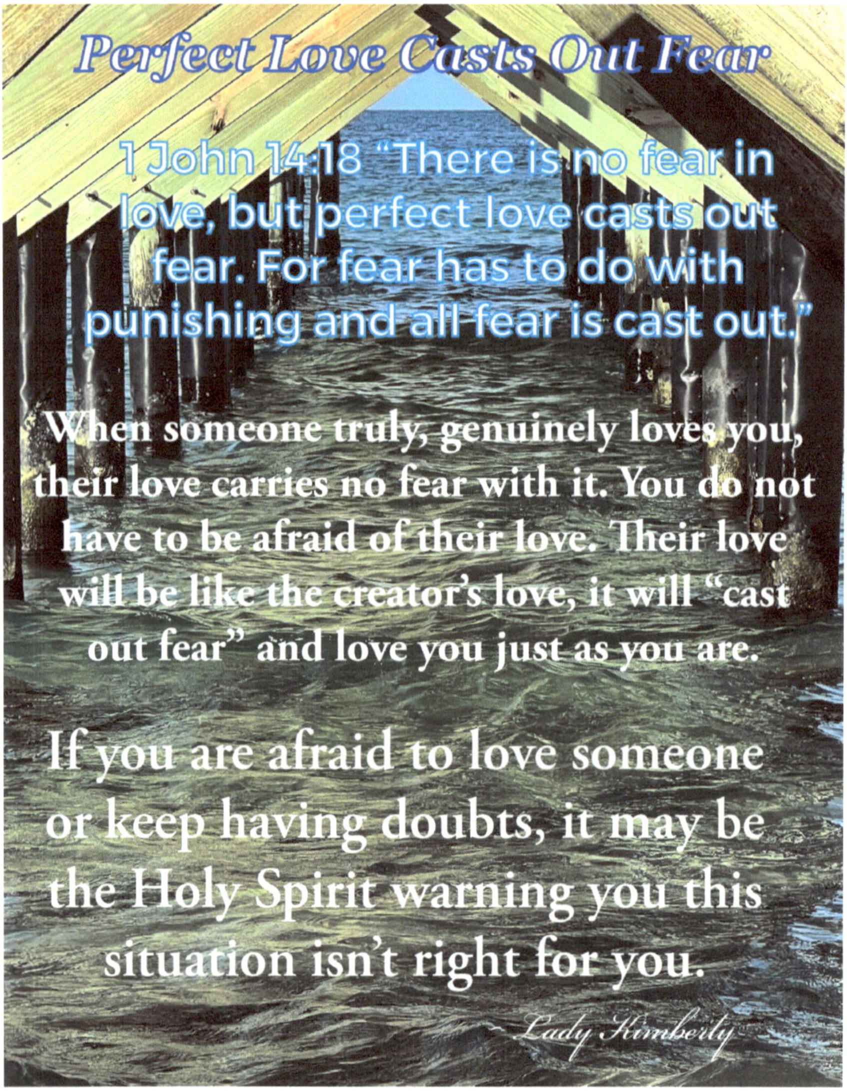

I KNEW YOU BEFORE YOU WERE BORN

For Anyone that has ever been told you don't have enough, you have too much, you aren't enough, you're not quite enough, you're just aren't quite what we are looking for....

YOU are exactly what God made YOU PERFECTLY for YOU to accomplish exactly what YOU want to accomplish.

Every step forward is a step NOT backwards

Even a tiny step is PROGRESS

Every article, certification, person you meet has something of value uniquely for YOU

Jeremiah 1:5, it tells us that our Creator knew us before we were born and that we were consecrated and appointed a prophet to the nations. To Consecrate is to bless, make holy or to dedicate to a higher purpose. To be appointed a prophet is to be asked to faithfully speak God's Word to the people.

So before we were ever born, we were blessed and made holy and we were asked to faithfully speak God's Word to the people.

The Hebrew word for "holy", kodesh, comes from the root word "Kadash". In simpler terms, it means to be set apart for a specific purpose. In this context, it means our Creator created us "for a specific purpose". Kind of cool isn't it? God knew us before we were born, He blessed us before we were born, He made us holy before we were born, meaning He created us for a very specific purpose He had in mind for each of us, and He asked us to faithfully speak His word to everyone we meet. And he did all of this before we were even born.

For me, I absolutely love knowing I was created for a "specific purpose", not just ON purpose but for a "specific purpose". God knows me. He knew me long before I was born. He knows you. He knew you long before you were born. He created each of us for a specific purpose. He blessed us. He made us Holy. He dedicated us to a higher purpose. God did all of this long before we were ever born. Isn't that just the coolest thing?

The next time you are feeling a little lost or hopeless, wondering what you are supposed to be doing with your life, remember this: God knows you. He knew you long before you were ever born. He created you for a purpose. He blessed you. He made you Holy. He dedicated you to a higher purpose, He asked you to faithfully speak His word to everyone you meet. Your life has a purpose. Your life had a purpose long before you were ever born!

Jeremiah 1:5, Before I formed you in the womb I knew you, and before you were born I consecrated you; I appointed you a prophet to the nations.

From "A Godly Way of Life" by Lady Kimberly Motes Doty

FOR I KNOW THE PLANS I HAVE FOR YOU

"For I know the plans I have for you," declares the LORD,
"plans to prosper you and not to harm you, plans to give
you hope and a future.", Jeremiah 29:11
- Lady Kimberly

MOVE ON, LET GO, IT'S OK

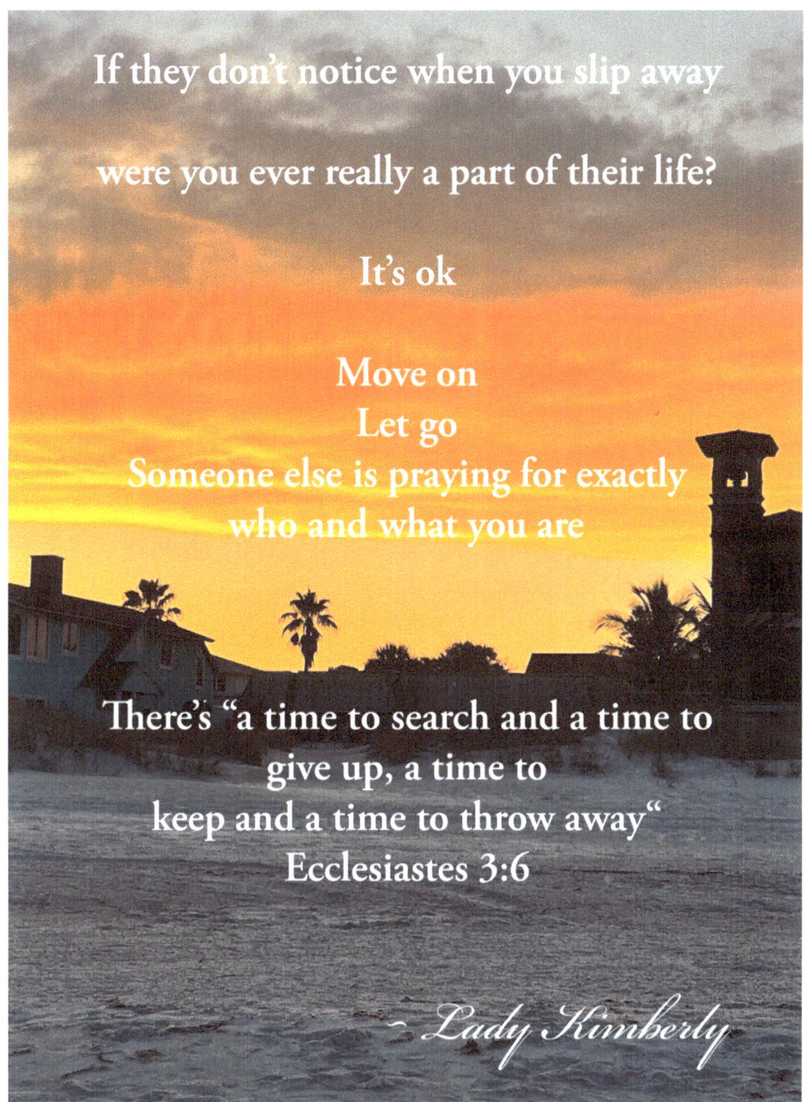
If they don't notice when you slip away
were you ever really a part of their life?
It's ok
Move on
Let go
Someone else is praying for exactly
who and what you are
There's "a time to search and a time to
give up, a time to
keep and a time to throw away"
Ecclesiastes 3:6
~ Lady Kimberly

IF YOU HAVE FAITH AS A GRAIN OF MUSTARD SEED

Matthew 17:20 … and Jesus said: for verily I say unto you, If ye have faith as a grain of mustard seed, ye shall say unto this mountain, Remove hence to yonder place; and it shall remove; and nothing shall be impossible unto you.

Jeremiah 29:11 ESV , "For I know the plans I have for you," declares the LORD, "plans to prosper you and not to harm you, plans to give you hope and a future."

Jesus was the originator of the Law of Attraction. What we believe, we achieve. Believing with all of our heart is the key to the love we desire and the life we want. When you truly believe it with all your heart, it is yours and always has been from before the beginning of time.

- Lady Kimberly

GOD WILL COMMAND HIS ANGELS CONCERNING YOU

For God will give command his angels concerning you to guard you in all your ways. Psalms 91:11
For it is written, "He will command his angels concerning you to guard you carefully:" Luke 4:10
~ Lady Kimberly

WITHOUT LOVE, I AM NOTHING

Without Love, I am Nothing
If I speak in the tongues of men
and of angels,
but have not love,
I am a noisy gong
or a clanging cymbal.
And if I have prophetic powers,
and understand all mysteries
and all knowledge,
and if I have all faith,
so as to remove mountains,
but have not love,
I am nothing.
If I give away all I have,
and if I deliver up my body to be burned,
but have not love,
I gain nothing.
1 Corinthians 13:1-3
- Lady Kimberly

LOVE IS...

Love is patient and kind;
love does not envy or boast;
it is not arrogant or rude.
It does not insist on its own way;
it is not irritable or resentful;
it does not rejoice at wrongdoing,
but rejoices with the truth.
Love bears all things,
believes all things,
hopes all things,
endures all things.
Love never ends.
As for prophecies,
they will pass away;
as for tongues,
they will cease;
as for knowledge,
it will pass away.
1 Corinthians 13:4-8
Love is …
~ Lady Kimberly

THE GREATEST OF THESE IS LOVE

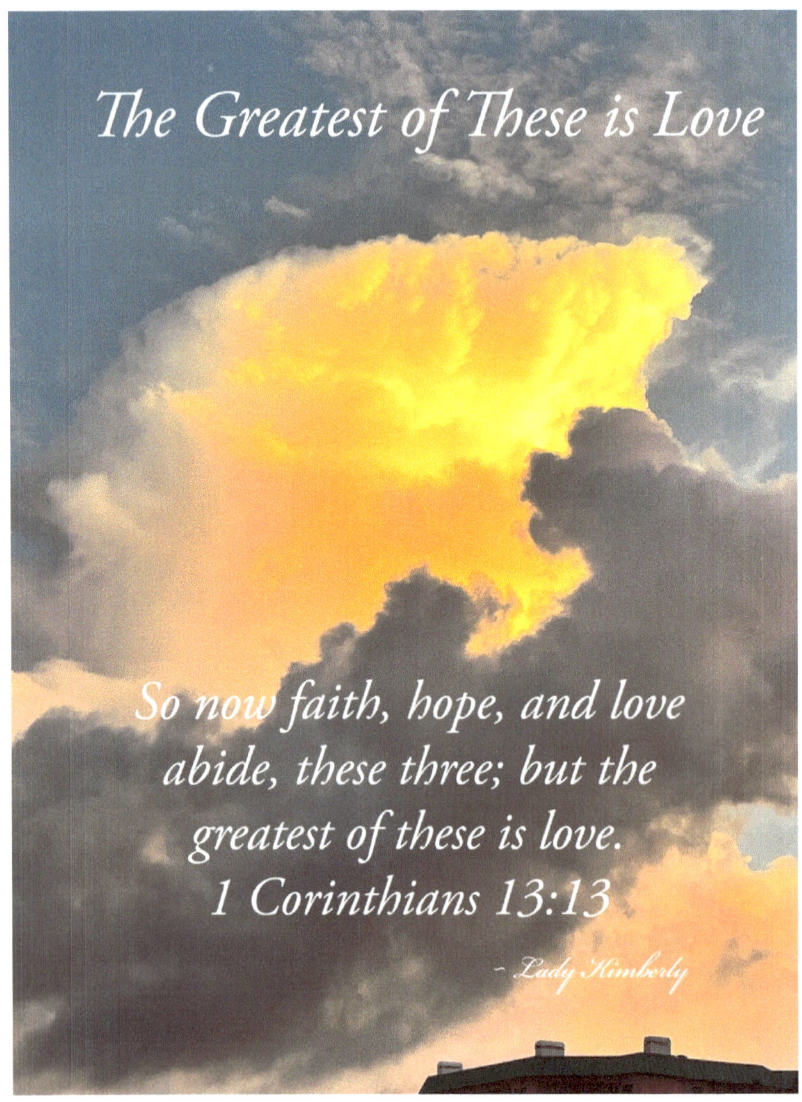
The Greatest of These is Love
So now faith, hope, and love
abide, these three; but the
greatest of these is love.
1 Corinthians 13:13
~ Lady Kimberly

DO EVERYTHING FOR LOVE

Let all that you do
be done in love.
1 Corinthians 16:14
~ Lady Kimberly

TRUST IN THE LORD TO RENEW YOUR STRENGTH

"But they that wait upon the LORD shall renew their strength;
they shall mount up with wings as eagles;
they shall run, and not be weary;
and they shall walk, and not faint."
Isaiah 40:31
- Lady Kimberly

BELIEVE IT & YOU HAVE RECEIVED IT

Believe it & You have Received it
Therefore I tell you,
whatever you ask for in prayer,
believe that you have received it,
and it will be yours.
Mark 11:24
~ Lady Kimberly

FAITH IS

Now faith is
confidence in what
we hope for
and assurance about
what we do not see.
Hebrews 11:1
~ Lady Kimberly

ABOVE ALL THESE PUT ON LOVE

above all these put on love,
which binds everything
in perfect harmony.
Colossians

THE KEY TO RECEIVING IS BELIEVING

The Key to Receiving is Believing
And all things, whatsoever ye shall ask in prayer, believing, ye shall receive.
Matthew 21:22
~ Lady Kimberly

BE THE EXAMPLE, NOT JUST THE VOICE

Be the example not just the voice
Do not merely listen to the word,
and so deceive yourselves.
Do what it says.
James 1:22
- Lady Kimberly

ABOVE ALL, LOVE EACH OTHER DEEPLY

Above All, Love Each Other Deeply
Above all,
love each other deeply,
because love covers over a
multitude of sins.
1 Peter 4:8
- Lady Kimberly

WITHOUT FAITH

Without Faith It Is Impossible to Please God
And without faith
it is impossible to please God,
because anyone who comes to him
must believe that he exists
and that he rewards those
who earnestly seek him.
Hebrews 11:6
~ Lady Kimberly

DO YOU HEAR WHAT I HEAR?

So faith comes from hearing,
and hearing
through the word of Christ.
Romans 10:17
Lady Kimberly

STRONG AND COURAGEOUS

"Be strong and courageous. Do not be afraid or
terrified because of them, for the Lord your God goes
with you; he will never leave you nor forsake you."
Deuteronomy 31:16
- Lady Kimberly

WALK BY FAITH

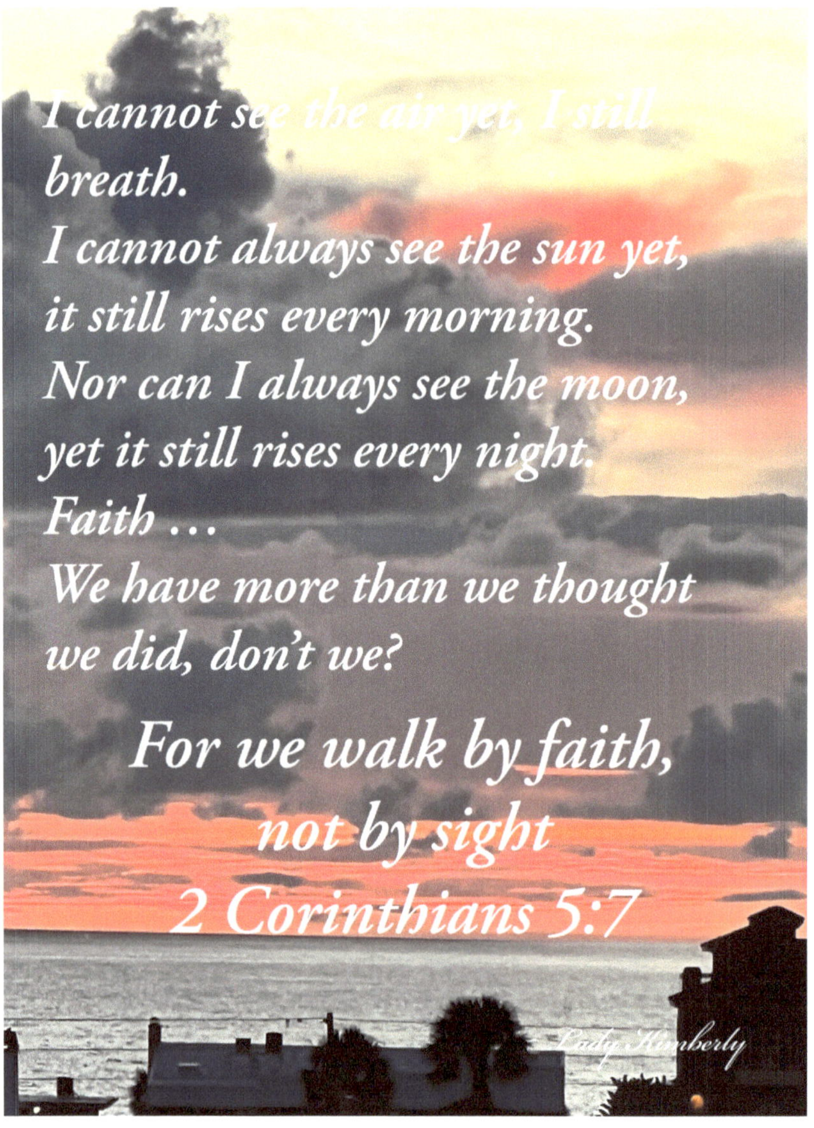
I cannot see the air yet, I still
breath.
I cannot always see the sun yet,
it still rises every morning.
Nor can I always see the moon,
yet it still rises every night.
Faith …
We have more than we thought
we did, don't we?
For we walk by faith,
not by sight
2 Corinthians 5:7
Lady Kimberly

WAIT PATIENTLY

But if we hope for
what we do not yet
have, we wait for it
patiently.
Romans 8:25
~ Lady Kimberly

Relationship

Inspirations

IT'S FOR MY OWN GOOD

I CAN CUT YOU OFF
AND STILL LOVE YOU
I CAN STOP SPEAKING TO YOU
AND STILL CARE FOR YOU
IF I LEAVE YOU ALONE,
IT'S NOT TO BE BITTER OR PETTY,
IT'S FOR MY OWN GOOD,
IF I LET YOU GO,
IT'S BECAUSE I NEED TO BE HAPPY,
WITH OR WITHOUT YOU
IN MY LIFE ...

SOMEONE WHO WON'T LET YOU FACE IT ALONE

DON'T LOOK FOR SOMEONE WHO WILL SOLVE ALL OF YOUR
LIFE'S PROBLEMS,
LOOK FOR SOMEONE WHO WON'T LET YOU FACE ANY OF
THEM ALONE.
~ LADY KIMBERLY
THE LIFE COACHING PLACE

IF I'M NOT YOUR EVERYTHING

If I'm not your everything,
I'm not your anything.

WITH THE RIGHT ONE

With the wrong one
It feels like you can't
do anything right,
Love is
Blind
With the right one,
It feels like you can't
do anything wrong...
~ Lady Kimberly

IF SHE IS AMAZING, SHE WON'T BE EASY

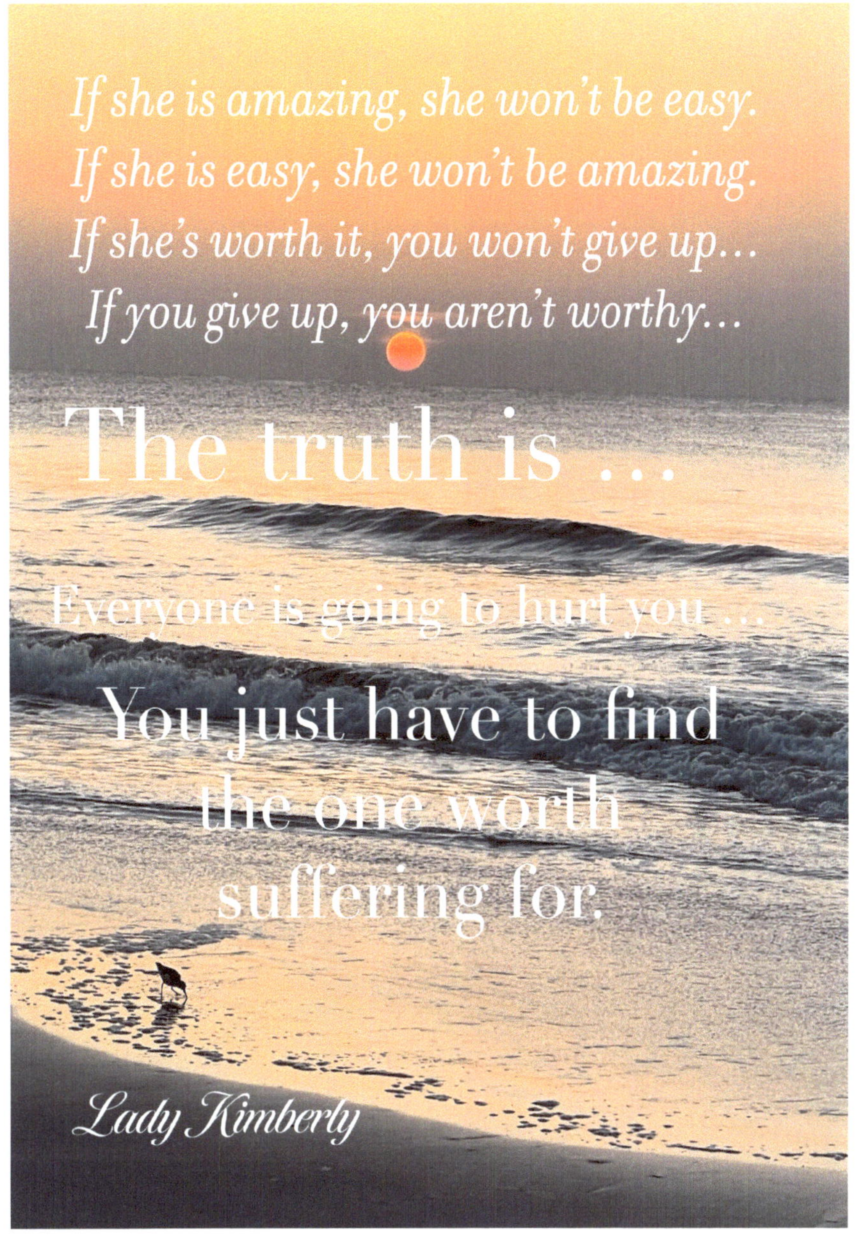
If she is amazing, she won't be easy.
If she is easy, she won't be amazing.
If she's worth it, you won't give up...
If you give up, you aren't worthy...
The truth is ...
Everyone is going to hurt you ...
You just have to find
the one worth
suffering for.
Lady Kimberly

IF SHE IS AMAZING, SHE WON'T BE EASY 2

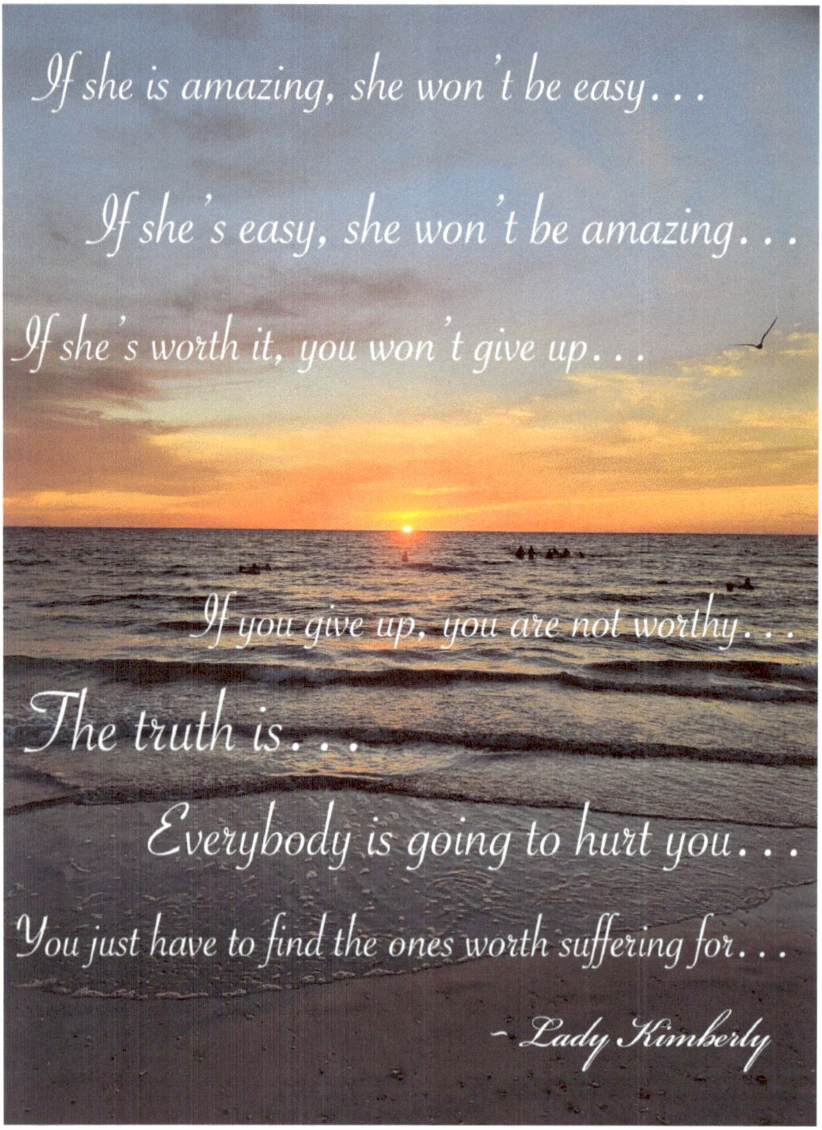

If she is amazing, she won't be easy...

If she's easy, she won't be amazing...

If she's worth it, you won't give up...

If you give up, you are not worthy...

The truth is...

Everybody is going to hurt you...

You just have to find the ones worth suffering for...

~Lady Kimberly

YOU ARE MY EVERYTHING

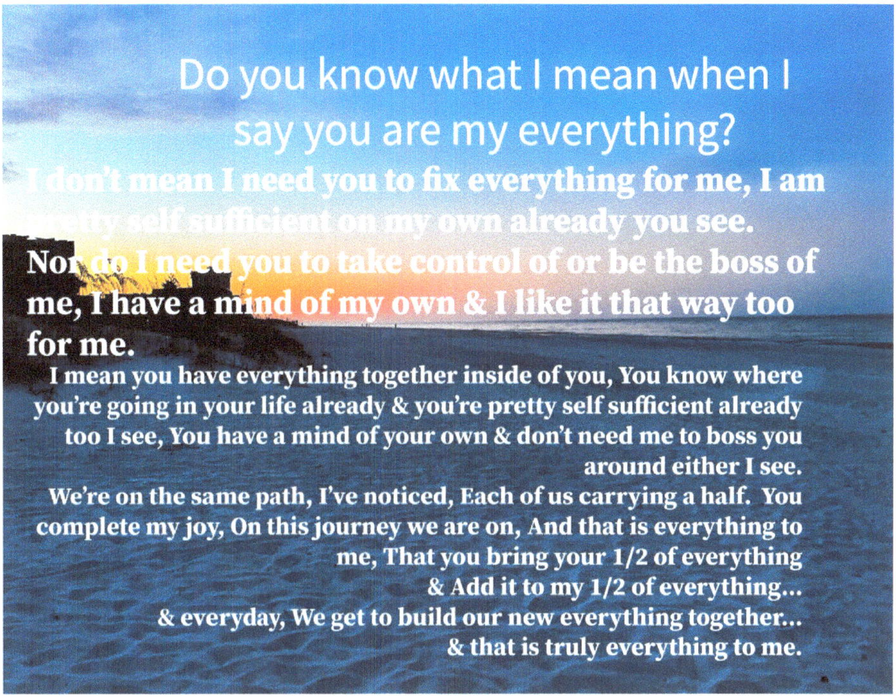

Do you know what I mean when I say you are my everything?

I don't mean I need you to fix everything for me, I am pretty self sufficient on my own already you see. Nor do I need you to take control of or be the boss of me, I have a mind of my own & I like it that way too for me.

I mean you have everything together inside of you, You know where you're going in your life already & you're pretty self sufficient already too I see, You have a mind of your own & don't need me to boss you around either I see.

We're on the same path, I've noticed, Each of us carrying a half. You complete my joy, On this journey we are on, And that is everything to me, That you bring your 1/2 of everything & Add it to my 1/2 of everything... & everyday, We get to build our new everything together... & that is truly everything to me.

EACH DAY BRINGS EVER CHANGING COLORS OF A NEW DAY

Each day our Creator brings us
the ever changing colors of the
new day as a sign of renewal . . .
Telling us each
day is a gift of
renewed
strength, hope
and a chance to
start again. . .
EVERY DAY IS YOUR
CHANCE AT A HAPPILY
EVER AFTER...
Just like the skies beautiful sunrise you have to be
brave enough to reach out each and every day and
grab it with both hands and make it your own
Lady Kimberly

EACH DAY BRINGS EVER CHANGING COLORS OF A NEW DAY2

Each day our Creator
brings us the ever
changing colors of the new
day as a sign of renewal ...
Telling us each day is a gift of
renewed strength, hope and a
chance to start again...
Every day is your
chance at a happily
ever after...
Just like the skies beautiful
sunrise you have to be brave
enough to reach out each and
every day and grab it with both
hands and make it your own.
Kimberly

INTIMACY IS

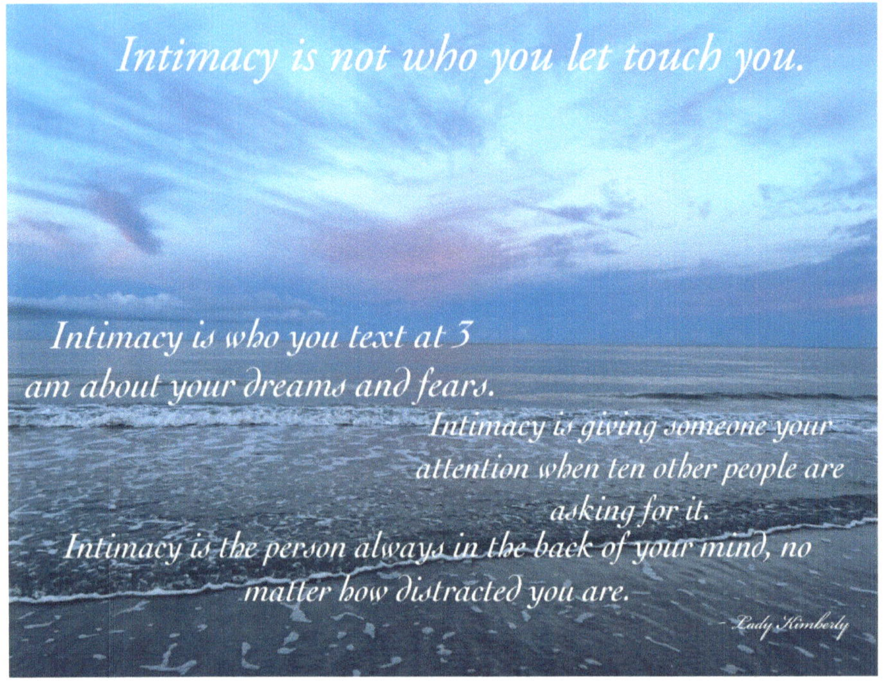
Intimacy is not who you let touch you.
Intimacy is who you text at 3 am about your dreams and fears.
Intimacy is giving someone your attention when ten other people are asking for it.
Intimacy is the person always in the back of your mind, no matter how distracted you are.
- Lady Kimberly

BE WITH SOMEONE WHO CHOOSES YOU EVERYDAY

Be with someone who chooses
you everyday not just when
they are in the mood for you.
Lady Kimberly

WHITE FEATHERS COME FROM THE PUREST ANGELS

White feathers come from the purest angels, and thus are messages of peace, love, protection and light… Finding a white feather is a powerful message and blessing from the Divine, and is a sign that all will be right for you soon…

By sharing this white feather of pure love, peace, protection, and light I am sharing a prayer with you to find your positivity and your ordained path for your life.

PEOPLE WHO ARE CRAZY ENOUGH

"People who are crazy
enough to think they
can change the world
are the ones who do."
Rob Siltanen
"Come get crazy
with me."
~ Lady Kimberly

PEOPLE WHO ARE CRAZY ENOUGH 2

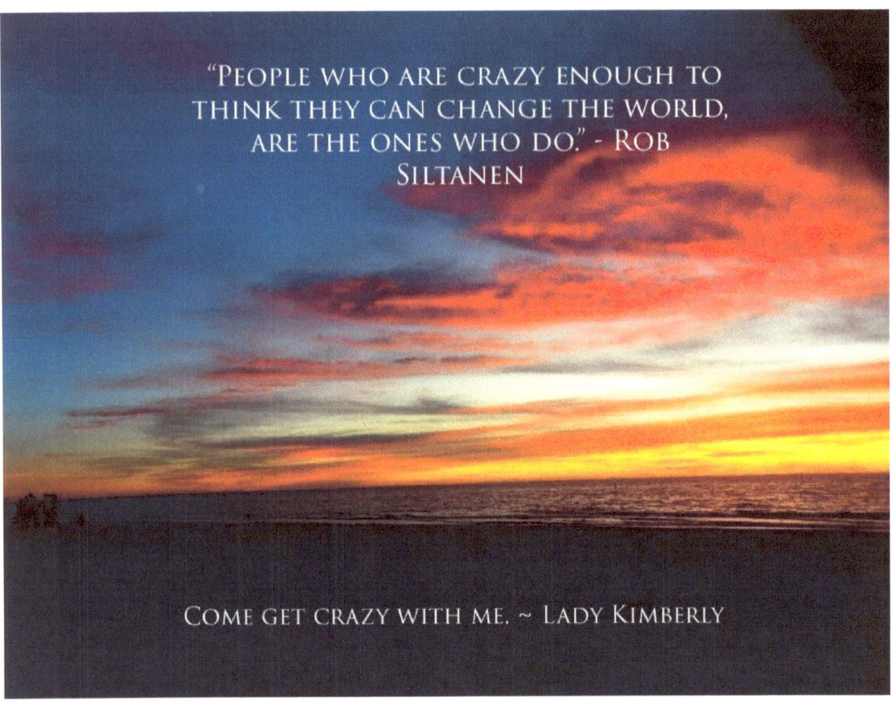
"People who are crazy enough to think they can change the world, are the ones who do." - Rob Siltanen
Come get crazy with me. ~ Lady Kimberly

YOU DESERVE SOMEONE

You deserve someone who texts you
boring little details of their day just so
they have a reason to talk to you.
~ Lady Kimberly

IT IS WHAT IT IS

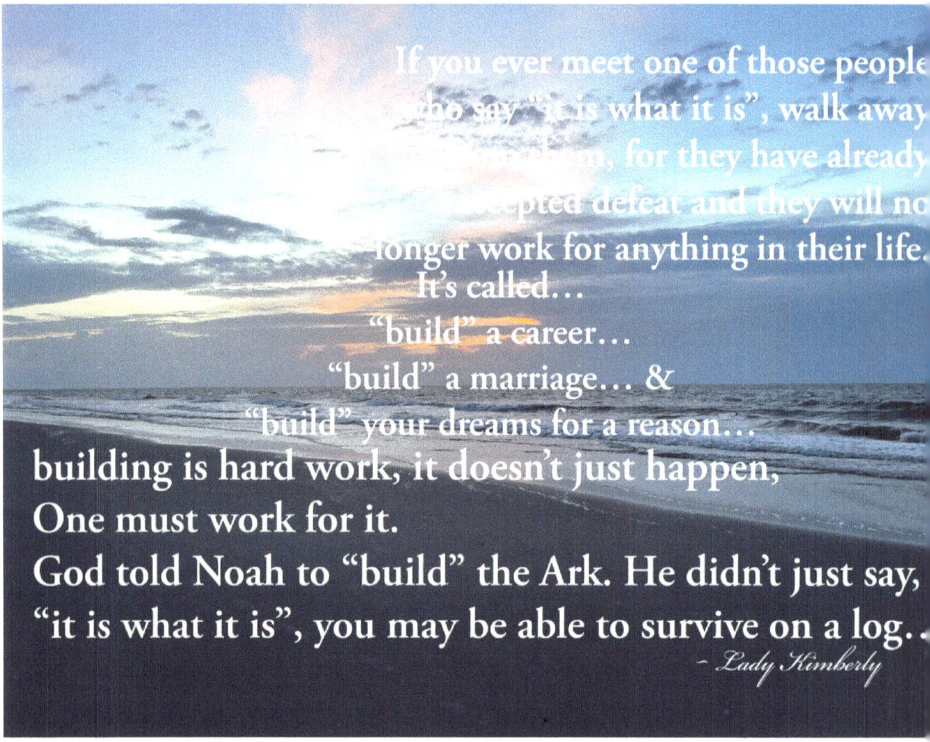

If you ever meet one of those peopl
who say "it is what it is", walk away
[illegible]m, for they have already
[illegible]pted defeat and they will no
longer work for anything in their life.
It's called…
"build" a career…
"build" a marriage… &
"build" your dreams for a reason…
building is hard work, it doesn't just happen,
One must work for it.
God told Noah to "build" the Ark. He didn't just say,
"it is what it is", you may be able to survive on a log..

~ *Lady Kimberly*

SOME PEOPLE CANNOT LOVE YOU

Some people cannot love you the way
you need to be loved because they are
emotionally and spiritually frozen.
They recoil from real affection and leave you in silence for days with no explanation. You will never meet a deep penetrating gaze from their shallow eyes, merely a surface glance. They can touch your hand with their hand, but never with their heart. They can serve your body but not your soul. They can only connect with you through utility but never passion. They are empty, dead inside.
They will break your heart if you let them. You will waste your whole life waiting for them to wake up to the treasure of what you have to offer if you stay, so walk away...
~ Lady Kimberly

SHE IS THE MOST MAGICAL

She is the most magical person I have ever met,
Having survived the most tragic story I have ever heard,
She is tragical...
Unknown.
~ Lady Kimberly

SHE FELL IN LOVE WITH GOD

She fell in love with God, and God
sent a man that fell in love with her.
Period. End of story. Unknown.
~ Lady Kimberly

PEOPLE WHO HAVE NO IDEA HOW WONDERFUL THEY ARE

I love people that have
no idea how wonderful
they are and go around
making the world a
better place.
- Lady Kimberly

12 RULES BY WHICH TO LIVE

12 Rules by Which to Live

1. Give yourself permission. You don't need anymore else's approval. You've got this.
2. Speak your mind respectfully from the heart. The real, no BS truth, sets you free.
3. Chase your dreams. Follow your own path. If the road less traveled makes your heart soar; it is the key to your happiness.
4. Show your real inner strength by giving kindness and compassion freely. Be the kindness and compassion you [illegible] see in the world.
5. Be fully responsible for your own happiness. No one else is responsible for [illegible] feel, think, or behave. You are strong enough to ask for help if you want or need [illegible]
6. Enjoy your own company. If a relationship isn't right, like yourself [illegible] solo.
7. Dance to your own rhythm. Care less about what others are doing and more about what is best for you.
8. Seek those that lift you up. Don't buy into the drama Mama. Toxic people, narcissists, and negative people only bring stress; avoid that mess.
9. Know how to take a compliment. One of the humblest acts of self love we can do is to accept a compliment with a simple 'Thank you'. It's not conceited or arrogant. Stop being your own worst critic.
10. Practice Boundary Club Rules. Create your own Boundary rules. Know what to accept and what to reject in people's behaviors and opportunities for your life. Break your boundary rules and you're out.
11. Make your own Rules. Carve your own path in life. Shatter stereotypes, glass ceilings, and molds. Forget what is expected; do what is necessary. Live your life your way to be happy, healthy, and wealthy.
12. Learn from your Mistakes. Have your own growth mindset. See what went wrong. Don't beat yourself up. Learn. Move on. As Edison said: I learned 1,000 ways not to make a light bulb. It only takes 1 right way to find success - find your success.

- Lady Kimberly, The Life Coaching Place

CHANGE YOUR MINDSET, CHANGE THE WORLD

Replace "Sorry's" with "Thank You's"
Instead of "Sorry I'm late"
Try "Thank you for waiting for me"
Change you mindset
Change your world
~ Lady Kimberly

IT'S MORE DIFFICULT TO REGRET

Never give up on something
you really want, it's difficult
to wait, but, it's more
difficult to regret ...
~ Lady Kimberly

MY REBELLIOUS LITTLE WILD CHILD

"My rebellious little wild child is ready to come
out and play today so I'm taking her on a Long
Beach walk accompanied by Eric Church,
Miranda Lambert, Jo ellencamp & others
like AWOL Nation th m to understand this
restlessness that come being isolated away
from our family and fr ds for way too long!"
Quotes from the pandemic - November 2020
~ Lady Kimberly

WHAT KIND OF FIRE ARE YOU?

Are you the kind of fire you burn with?

The kind you play with?

Or are you both?

The most important point is this:

Do not put out your fire because someone else doesn't understand your flame

IT'S ABOUT TIME

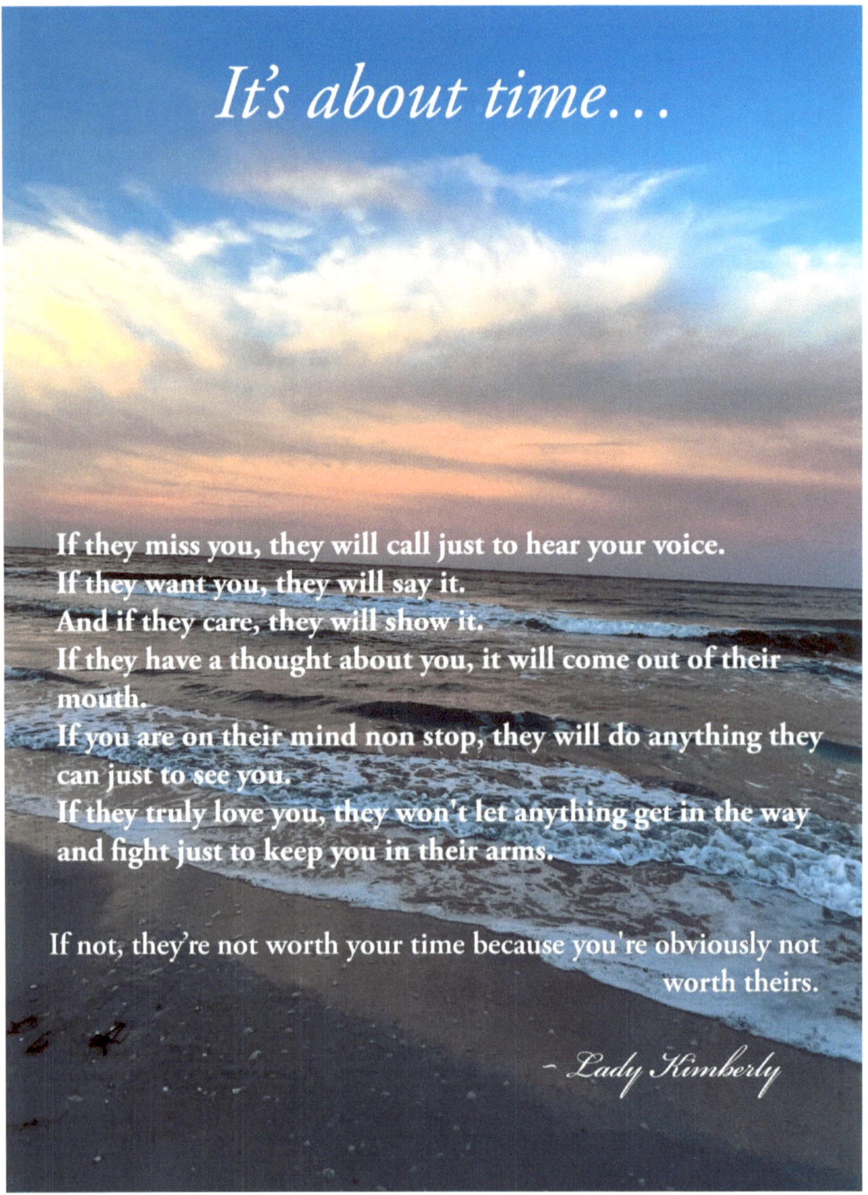
It's about time…
If they miss you, they will call just to hear your voice.
If they want you, they will say it.
And if they care, they will show it.
If they have a thought about you, it will come out of their mouth.
If you are on their mind non stop, they will do anything they can just to see you.
If they truly love you, they won't let anything get in the way and fight just to keep you in their arms.
If not, they're not worth your time because you're obviously not worth theirs.
~ Lady Kimberly

EVERYDAY IS YOUR CHANCE FOR A HAPPILY EVERAFTER

Everyday is your chance for
your happily ever after.
What are you doing today to
make yours happen?
~ Lady Kimberly

I AM WORTHY AFFIRMATION

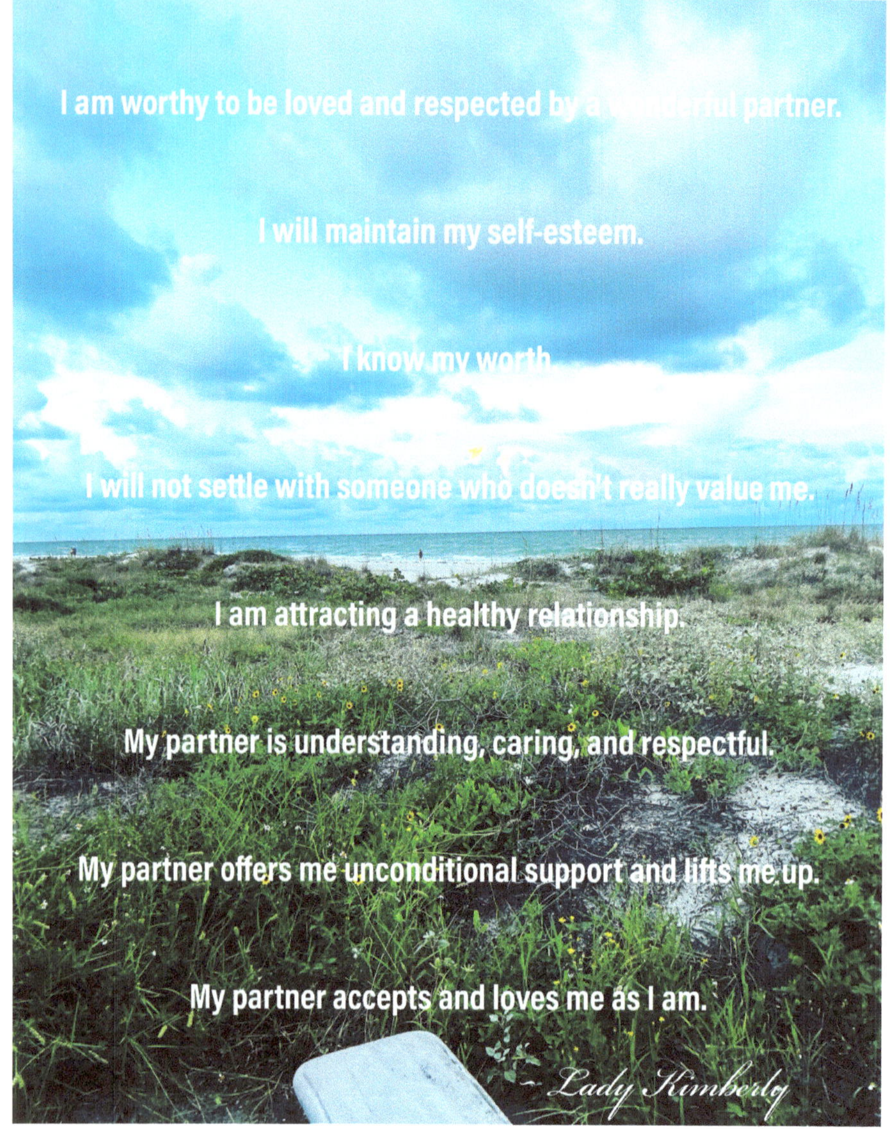
I am worthy to be loved and respected by a wonderful partner.
I will maintain my self-esteem.
I know my worth.
I will not settle with someone who doesn't really value me.
I am attracting a healthy relationship.
My partner is understanding, caring, and respectful.
My partner offers me unconditional support and lifts me up.
My partner accepts and loves me as I am.
~ Lady Kimberly

IMAGINE LIVING A LIFE SO FULL OF LIFE

Imagine living life so carefully that there are no signs you lived at all.
Raven Leilani

I cannot imagine it.
So I cannot live it.

I want to live a life so full of LIFE that even if it's just my great great great grand children, someone still talks about what an amazing crazy awesome risk taker in love, business, life this otherwise simple down to earth woman was.

~ *Lady Kimberly*

I LOVE KIND PEOPLE

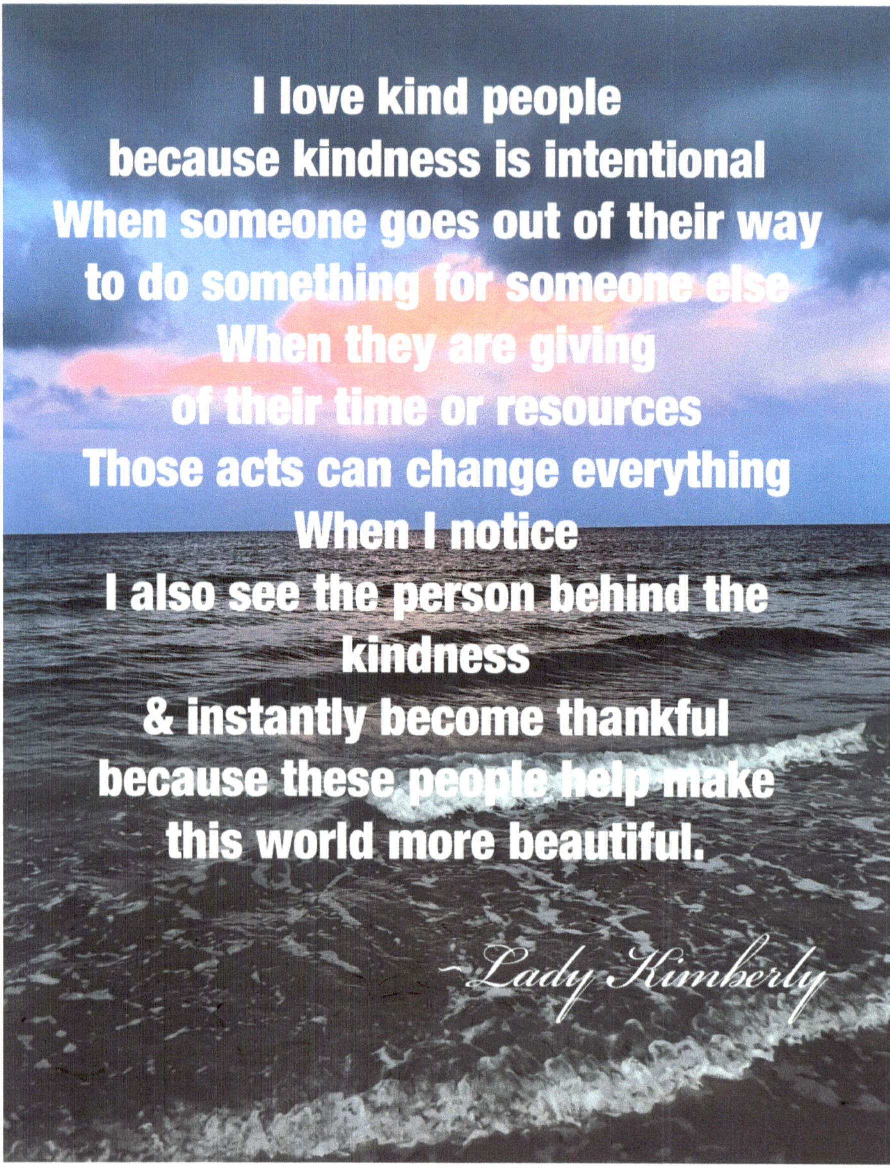

I love kind people
because kindness is intentional
When someone goes out of their way
to do something for someone else
When they are giving
of their time or resources
Those acts can change everything
When I notice
I also see the person behind the
kindness
& instantly become thankful
because these people help make
this world more beautiful.

~Lady Kimberly

I LOVE THE INTENTIONALITY OF KIND PEOPLE

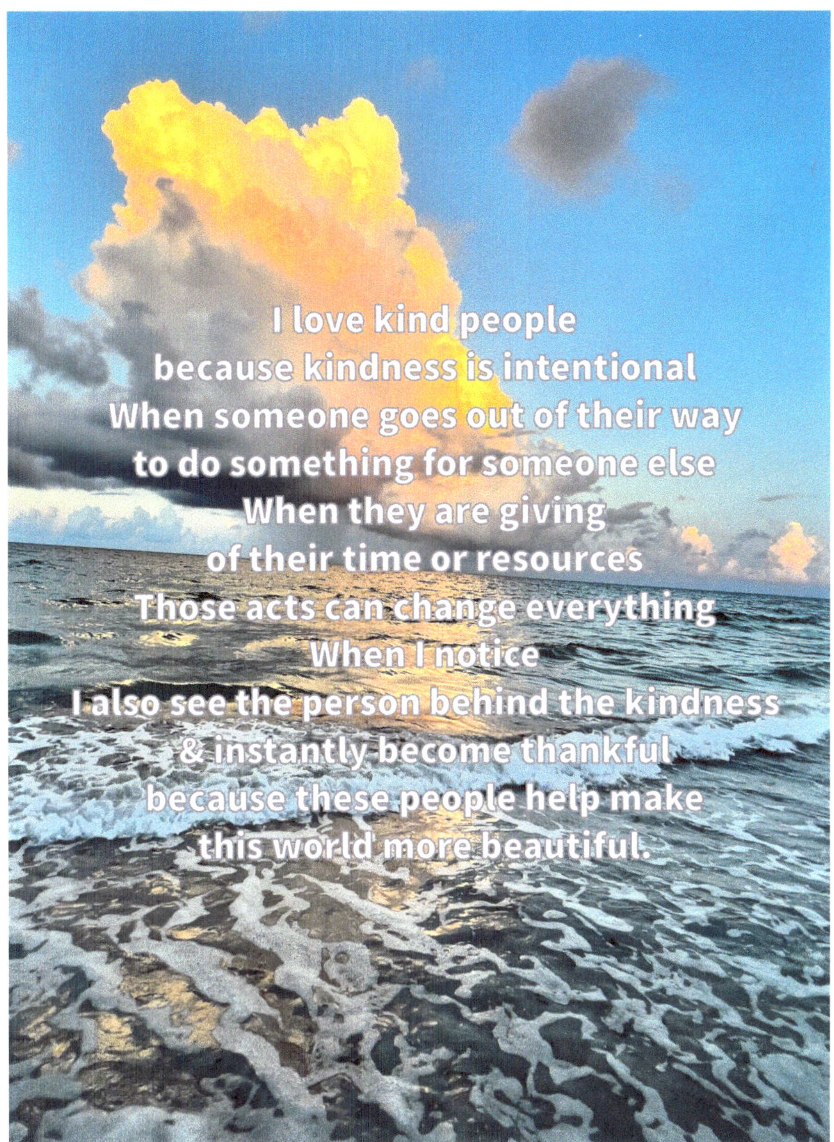

SOME MORNINGS LONELINESS PERMEATES

Some mornings loneliness
permeates every vibrant
color like my soul is echoing
the melancholy inside of me
like an intimate portrait out
into the world
~ Lady Kimberly

THE KIND OF LOVE THAD DOESN'T DEMAND

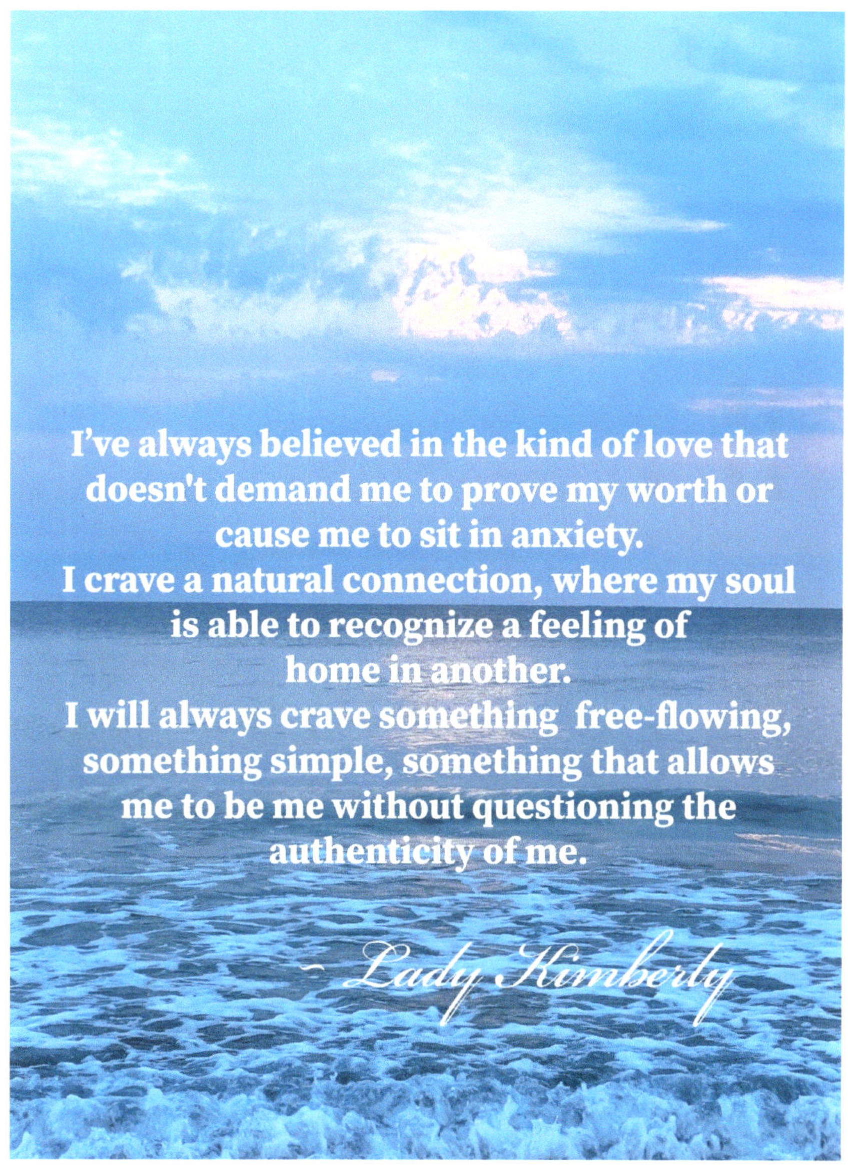
I've always believed in the kind of love that
doesn't demand me to prove my worth or
cause me to sit in anxiety.
I crave a natural connection, where my soul
is able to recognize a feeling of
home in another.
I will always crave something free-flowing,
something simple, something that allows
me to be me without questioning the
authenticity of me.
~ Lady Kimberly

I TRIED TO CATCH THE MOON TODAY

I tried to catch the moon today
But the clouds came & took her away
So I walked on into the painted sky
Before it too could say goodbye

~ Lady Kimberly

I TRIED TO CATCH THE MOON TODAY 2

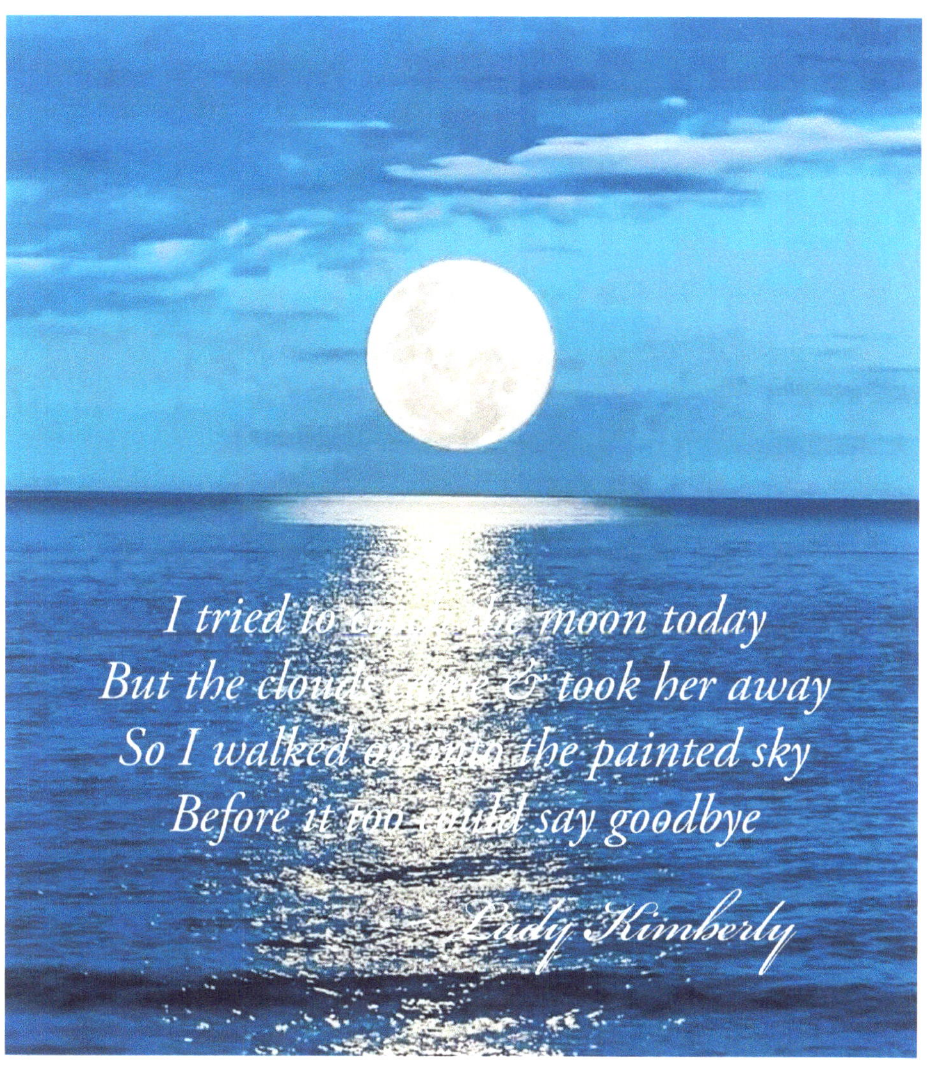
I tried to catch the moon today
But the clouds came & took her away
So I walked on into the painted sky
Before it too could say goodbye
Lady Kimberly

I AM THE WILDFIRE

I am the wildfire from which all other flames ignite
I am the wild flower others search the world to
plant in their gardens only to find
I only grow in the wild
I am the will of iron that pulls you through the
darkest moments of your soul just to find me
I am that which you have kept hidden within
I am you: I am not
I am that which was sent to live within
I am the queen of all queens
And the king of all kings
I am that hope that helped hold you together when
everything else fell apart
I am the reason you were stronger than you ever
thought and wiser than you ever knew you could be
I am all that has ever been known
And all that will ever be
I am the soul of all eternity.

Lady Kimberly

CLEARING AWAY ALL NEGATIVITY

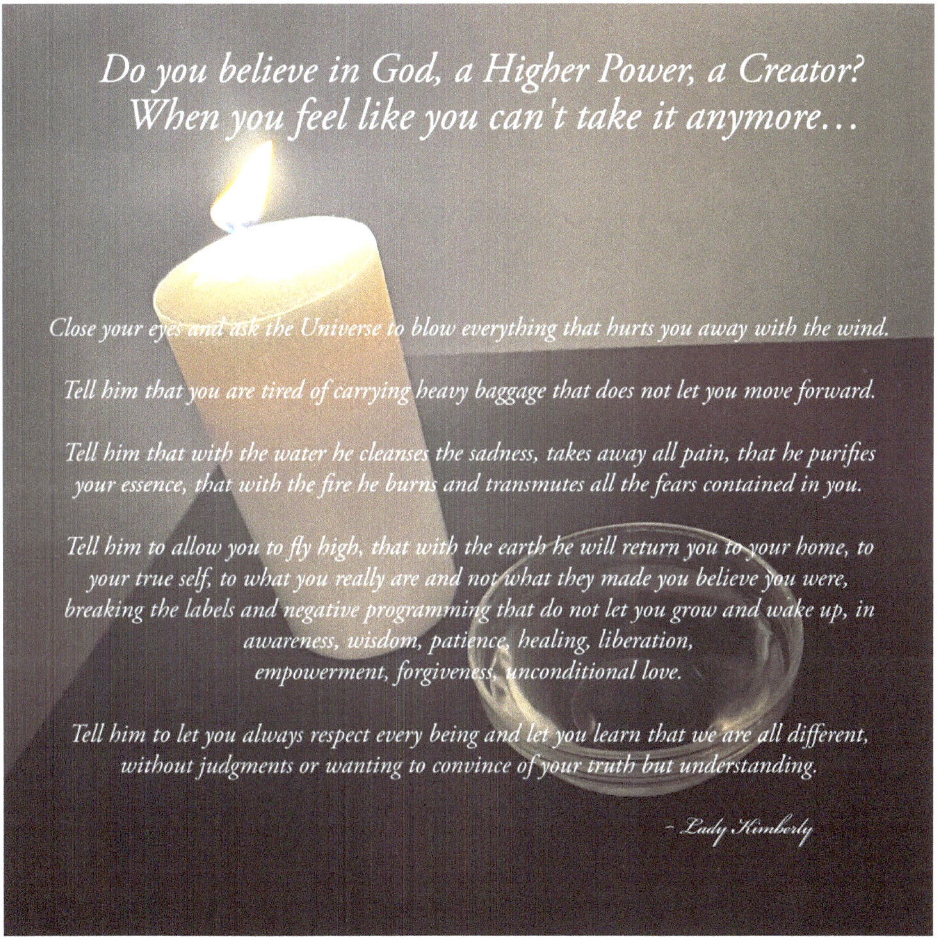

Do you believe in God, a Higher Power, a Creator?
When you feel like you can't take it anymore…

Close your eyes and ask the Universe to blow everything that hurts you away with the wind.

Tell him that you are tired of carrying heavy baggage that does not let you move forward.

Tell him that with the water he cleanses the sadness, takes away all pain, that he purifies your essence, that with the fire he burns and transmutes all the fears contained in you.

Tell him to allow you to fly high, that with the earth he will return you to your home, to your true self, to what you really are and not what they made you believe you were, breaking the labels and negative programming that do not let you grow and wake up, in awareness, wisdom, patience, healing, liberation, empowerment, forgiveness, unconditional love.

Tell him to let you always respect every being and let you learn that we are all different, without judgments or wanting to convince of your truth but understanding.

- Lady Kimberly

LIVE A LIFE THAT MATTERS

Live a life that matters.
Live a life of love.
~ Lady Kimberly

WHEN THE SOUL IS SET FREE

When the soul has been set free,
we don't ask why…
We simply say
May it always be …
~ Lady Kimberly

IS IT REALLY WORTH YOUR TIME?

Some people just
want the attention of having
you without the responsibility
of being committed to you.
Is it really worth your time to
give them your time?
Lady Kimberly

I COULD NEVER GROW TIRED OF THIS

I could never even in a
million years grow
tired of this...
Lady Kimberly

YOU ARE ENOUGH AS YOU ARE

You are enough, As you are…

Someone right now is asking God for someone
exactly like you…

The way you smile,
the way you cry,
the way you
the way you
the real You..

Because You are enough, just as you are…

It's Okay to walk away from anyone who tears
you down & makes you think otherwise…

~ *Lady Kimberly*

CELEBRATE & DANCE IN THE BLESSINGS

Some will only ever see
the gloom of the foggy day
While others will celebrate
and dance in the blessings of
the angel's wings God has
sprinkled all around them
- Lady Kimberly

WONDERWOMAN WHISPERED TO SUPERMAN

WonderWoman whispered to Superman…
Take me on the
ride of our lives

I REFUSE TO GO BACK TO SLOW DEATH

I refuse to go back to a tame love with Careful touches and Shallow kissing full of Faint words of interest or caring. I've been there, done that. It's not for me. There's such a lack of passion that it's a sure way to boredom and a
slow way to death.

I need to own, claim, claw, bite, and grab. To feel with my gut. I need out of breath, sloppy, rough kisses and sweaty bodies craving each other. I want to hear in no uncertain terms that I'm the only one as I grab him to look into my eyes when I tell him how much I absolutely love him. I want unleashed passion, unbridled desire and an inferno of need that is downright impossible to douse. My love is savage, raw untamed and territorial. It's so unreasonable that for the right man it makes perfect sense. It's so intense it seems impossible to keep up with, but he will know that my love is the only love he deserves and he will protect it just as territorially as I do.

~ *Lady Kimberly*

SILENCE IS A CHASM

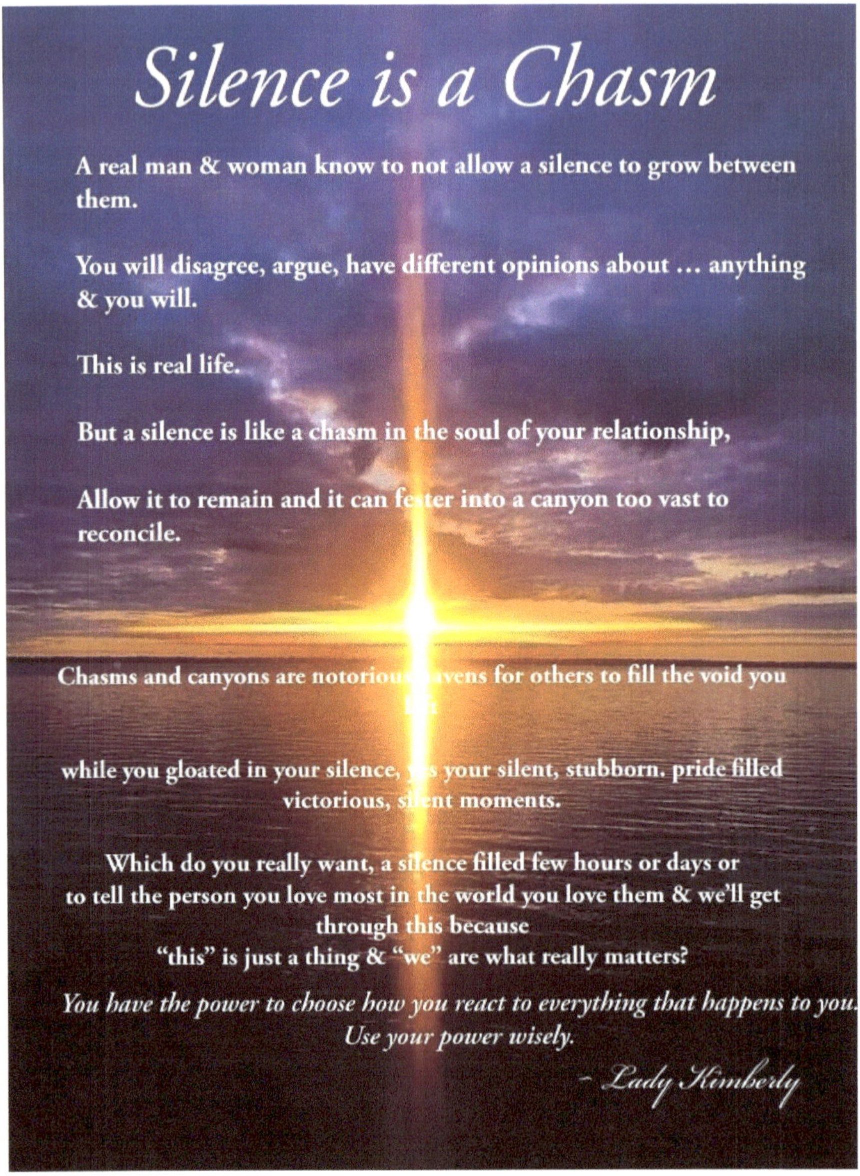

Silence is a Chasm

A real man & woman know to not allow a silence to grow between them.

You will disagree, argue, have different opinions about … anything & you will.

This is real life.

But a silence is like a chasm in the soul of your relationship,

Allow it to remain and it can fester into a canyon too vast to reconcile.

Chasms and canyons are notorious havens for others to fill the void you left

while you gloated in your silence, yes your silent, stubborn, pride filled victorious, silent moments.

Which do you really want, a silence filled few hours or days or to tell the person you love most in the world you love them & we'll get through this because "this" is just a thing & "we" are what really matters?

You have the power to choose how you react to everything that happens to you. Use your power wisely.

~ Lady Kimberly

I DON'T LOVE CASUALLY

I Don't Love Casually

I don't love casually
When I choose to love
I love fiercely
It's my soul ripped wide open & raw
it's my whole heart on display
It's all I have and everything I know on display
Handed over to you as a gift
And I hope you have the respect
To open it gently
And love me back
Just as fiercely
With your soul ripped wide open & raw
And your whole heart on display
With everything you have and everything you know
on display
as your gift back to me
And I promise
I will open it gently
For all eternity to see
I belong to you
Just as you belong to me

~ Lady Kimberly

If I'm not your everything
I'm not your anything.

IT IS TIME TO JUST BE HAPPY

It is time to just be happy.
Being angry, sad and
overthinking isn't worth it
anymore.
Just let things flow.
Be positive.
- Lady Kimberly

BREAK THE CYCLE

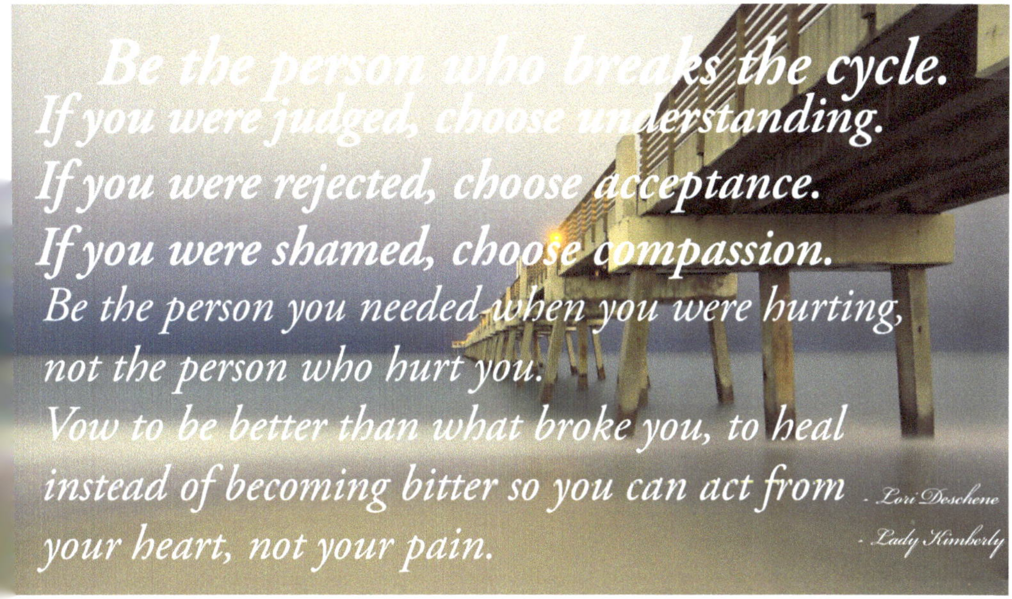

Be the person who breaks the cycle.
If you were judged, choose understanding.
If you were rejected, choose acceptance.
If you were shamed, choose compassion.
Be the person you needed when you were hurting, not the person who hurt you.
Vow to be better than what broke you, to heal instead of becoming bitter so you can act from your heart, not your pain.

- Lori Deschene
- Lady Kimberly

THEY KNEW EXACTLY WHAT THEY WERE DOING

They knew exactly what they were doing to you.

And what is even harder is…
The fact they knew and yet, they still went along with it.
Some people just don't care.
Some people will screw you over and act as if nothing happened. At all.

Or worse, that you did something wrong.

You did nothing wrong.

I FOUND MY PERSON

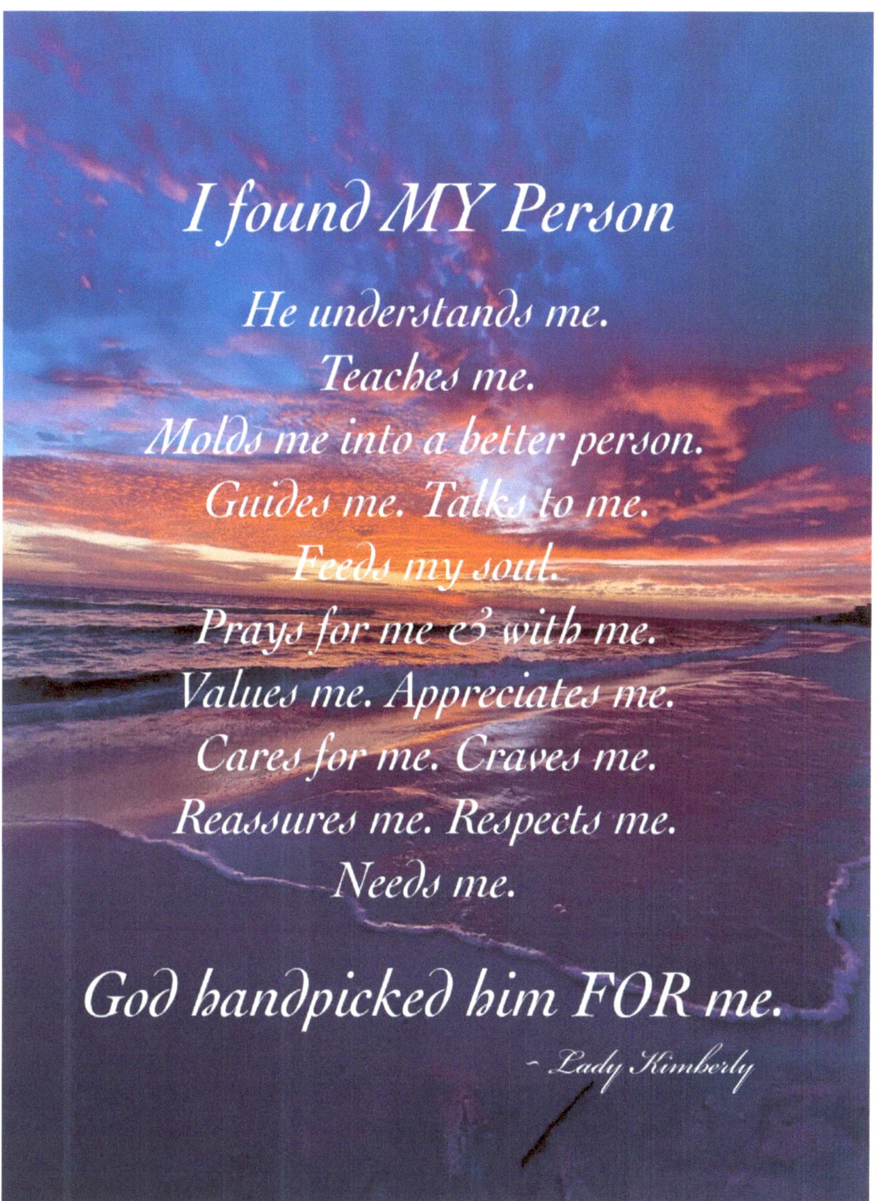
I found MY Person
He understands me.
Teaches me.
Molds me into a better person.
Guides me. Talks to me.
Feeds my soul.
Prays for me & with me.
Values me. Appreciates me.
Cares for me. Craves me.
Reassures me. Respects me.
Needs me.
God handpicked him FOR me.
~ Lady Kimberly

A BROKEN DREAM IS SHARPER THAN GLASS

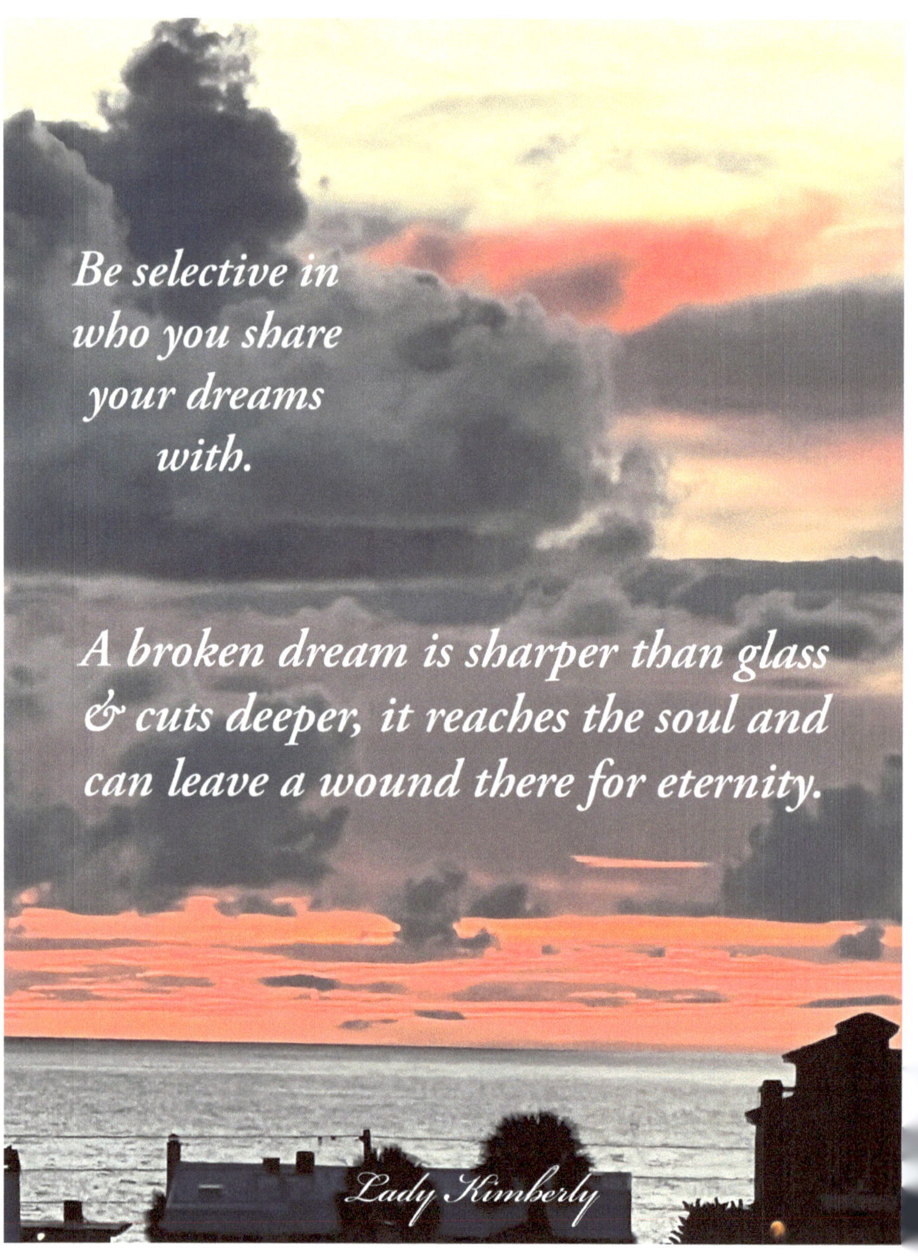
Be selective in
who you share
your dreams
with.
A broken dream is sharper than glass
& cuts deeper, it reaches the soul and
can leave a wound there for eternity.
Lady Kimberly

MAKE YOUR OWN ZEN

Make your own Zen
Finding your resting beach face daily means never having to worry about getting a resting bitch face ever again.

I COULDN'T REMEMBER THE LAST TIME

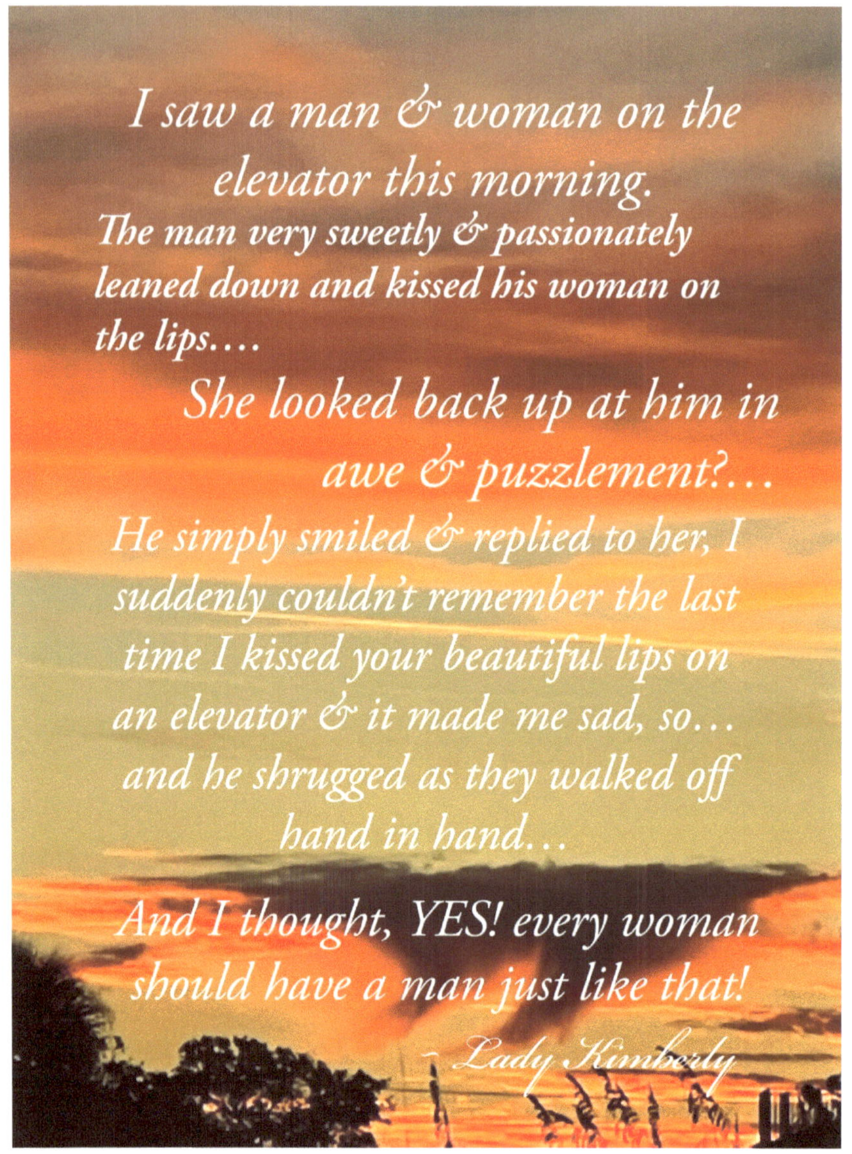
I saw a man & woman on the
elevator this morning.
The man very sweetly & passionately
leaned down and kissed his woman on
the lips....
She looked back up at him in
awe & puzzlement?...
He simply smiled & replied to her, I
suddenly couldn't remember the last
time I kissed your beautiful lips on
an elevator & it made me sad, so...
and he shrugged as they walked off
hand in hand...
And I thought, YES! every woman
should have a man just like that!
~ Lady Kimberly

COME GET CRAZY WITH ME

"People who are crazy
enough to think they can
change the world are the
ones who do. "
Rob Siltanen
"Come get crazy with me.
~ Lady Kimberly

LET'S CHANGE THE WORLD

"People who are crazy enough
to think they can change the
world are the ones who do. "
Rob Siltanen
"Come get crazy with me."
~ Lady Kimberly

THEY'RE NOT YOURS

If they pick a
fight with you
every Friday ...
That lasts
through every
Monday ...
Keep walking Hon,
they're not yours
anymore anyway ...
Lady Kimberly

10 WAYS TO BE YOUR BEST IRRESISTIBLE YOU

10 Ways to Be Your Best Irresistible You

1. Be Kind to everyone.
2. Know your worth.
3. Help everyone shine.
4. Avoid drama.
5. Share the credit.
6. Practice Collaboration not competition.
7. Be who you are.
8. Do or Do Not.
9. Make the extra effort.
10. Start each day with prayer.

~ Lady Kimberly

AN ELEGANT WOMAN

An Elegant Woman
1. Watches Her Language
2. Keeps Her Word
3. Watches Her Posture
4, Believes In Herself
5. Forms Her Own Opinions
6. Is Well Mannered
7. Maintains Her Composure
8. Is Modest 6 Polite
9. Empowers Other Women
10. Empowers Men
11. Fights For What She Believes In
12. Is Independent
13. Is Unapologetic About Herself
14. Believes in a Higher Power, God
Lady Kimberly

THE TWO SIDES OF MAN

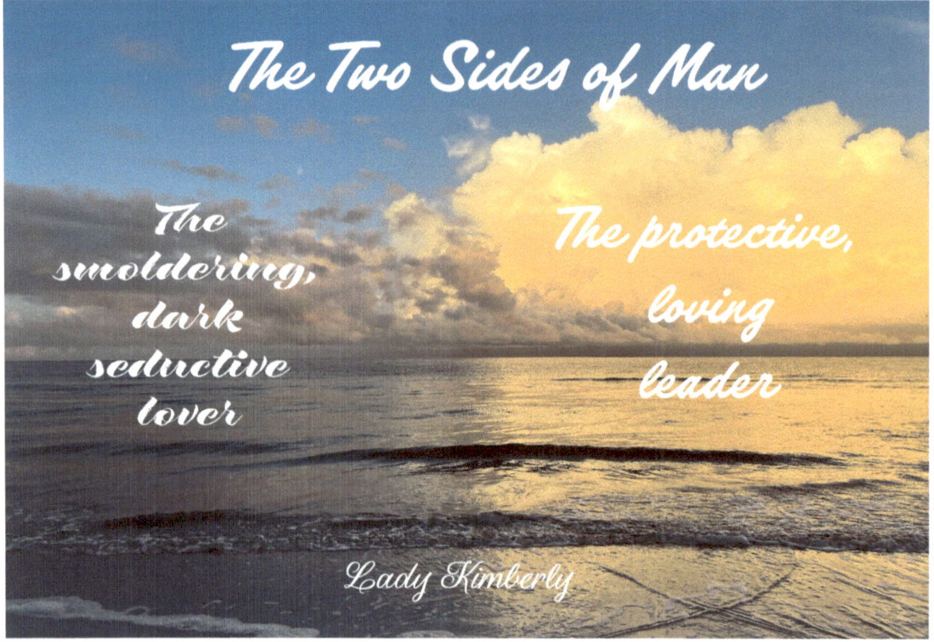
The Two Sides of Man
The smoldering, dark seductive lover
The protective, loving leader
Lady Kimberly

THE RIGHT ONE WILL LOVE YOU HARDER

Don't let anyone make
you believe its hard to
love you...
The right one will love
you harder than you
ever believed possible...
Lady Kimberly

A MAN IN LOVE

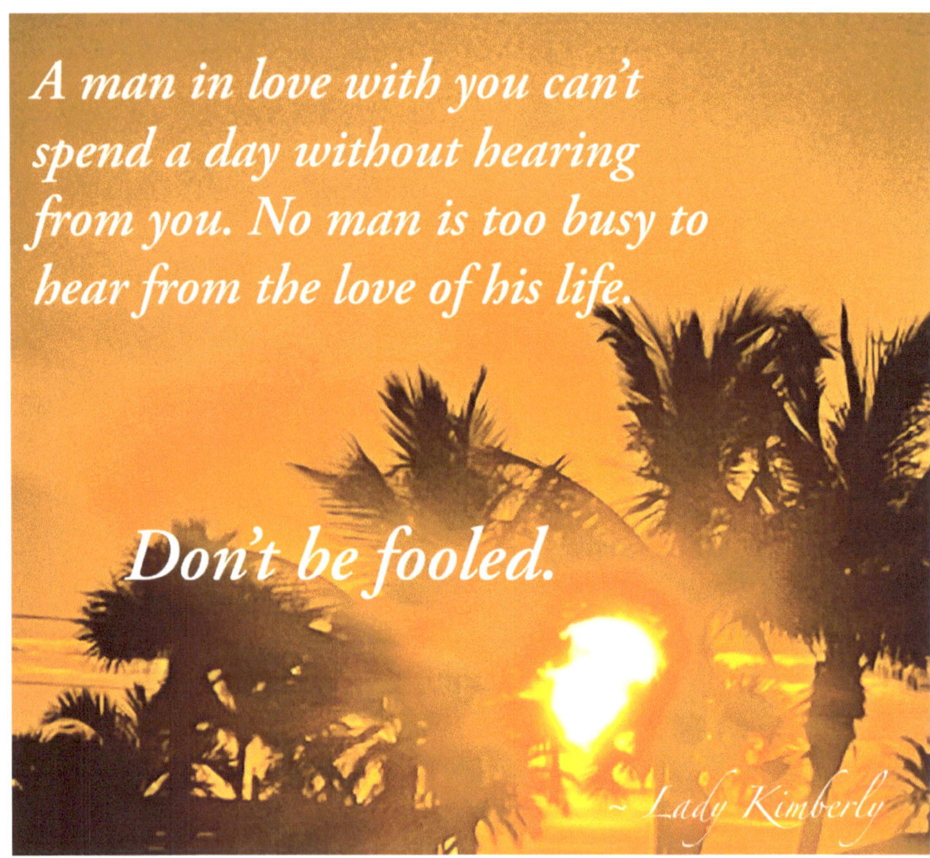
A man in love with you can't spend a day without hearing from you. No man is too busy to hear from the love of his life.
Don't be fooled.
~ Lady Kimberly

IN A WORLD FULL OF PROM QUEENS

In a world full of Prom Queens …
Find your inner Gypsy Mermaid & set her free, for she never ages …
Lady Kimberly

YOU KNOW YOU HAVE FOUND THE RIGHT ONE

You know you've found
the right one when
you're in the middle of
an argument and they
check on you to see it
you're Okay
... but still insist they're not
talking to you yet

7 THINGS EVERY WOMAN WANTS FROM HER MAN

7 Things Every Woman Wants from Her Man

1. Good Morning / Good Night texts
2. Hugs from behind
3. Deep / Long Conversations
4. Taking Pictures Together
5. Little Surprises
6. Saying why you love her
7. Making her a priority

- Lady Kimberly

ENDLESS LOVE IS FUELED BY

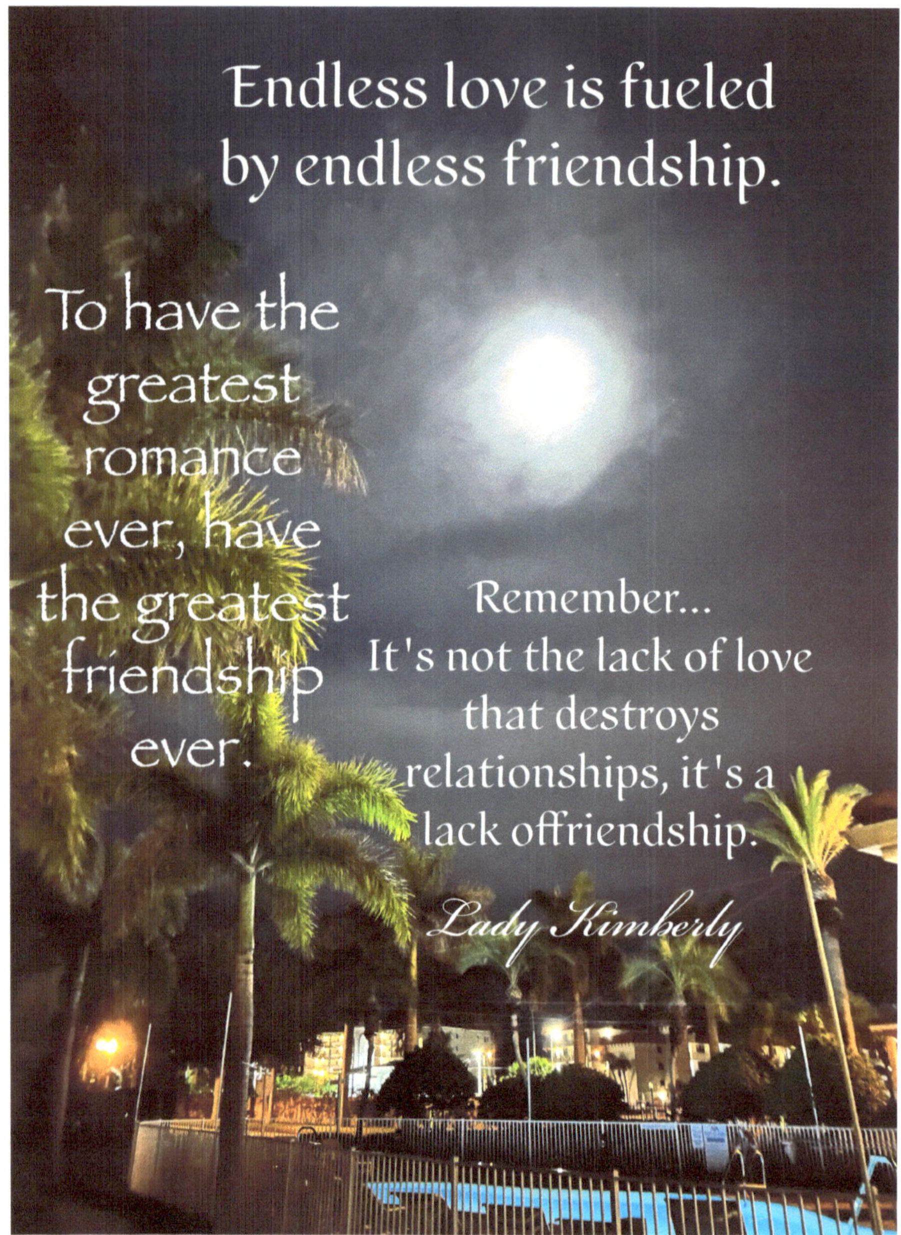
Endless love is fueled
by endless friendship.
To have the
greatest
romance
ever, have
the greatest
friendship
ever.
Remember...
It's not the lack of love
that destroys
relationships, it's a
lack offriendship.
Lady Kimberly

ARE YOU MOVING FORWARD OR STANDING STILL?

"Action is the foundational key to all success." - Pablo Picasso
"Motivation is the difference between moving forward and standing still. Find what motivates you." ~ Lady Kimberly

ARE YOU MOVING FORWARD OR STANDING STILL 2

"Action is the foundational key to all success."
- Pablo Picasso
"Motivation is the difference between moving forward and standing still. Find what motivates you." ~ Lady Kimberly

EVERYONE HAS THEIR OWN KIND OF BEAUTIFUL

Everyone has their own kind of beautiful,
Some are obvious, like a wild flower,
Or a California dream,
Others are like a wildfire,
Crazy & exotic.
Be your authentic beautiful,
Whatever your beautiful happens to be...
Flaunt it my lovely.
Someone out there is craving your
exact brand of beautiful.
Lady Kimberly

BELIEVE IN YOURSELF

BELIEVE IN YOURSELF
YOU ALREADY HAVE THE ANSWER
GOD GAVE IT TO YOU BEFORE YOU
WERE BORN

SPOIL ME ROYALLY

Spoil me...Royally...
Not just with a little of your money.
Spoil me with . . .
. . . your time
. . . your attention
. . . mentally
Spoil me with your love…
~ Lady Kimberly

YOU'RE THE REASON I …

You're the reason I …

Love
Trust
Believe
… Again

Blame it on me …

I love you
I trust you
I believe in you
… Always & Forever

~ Lady Kimberly

GIVE YOURSELF PERMISSION

1. Give yourself permission. You don't need anymore else's approval. You've got this.
2. Speak your mind respectfully from the heart . The real,
3. Chase your dreams, road less traveled makes your
4. Show your real inner strength freely. You never
know you've had days when
5. Be fully responsible for your own
6. Enjoy your own company. If a relationship isn't right, like yourself enough to
7. Dance to your own rhythm. Care less about what others are doing and more about what is
8. Seek those that lift you up. Don't buy into the drama Mama. Toxic people, narcissists, and negative people only bring stress; avoid
9. Know how to take a compliment. One of the humblest acts of self love we can do is to accept a compliment with a simple 'Thank you'. It's not conceited or arrogant. Stop being your own worst critic.
10. Practice Boundary Club Rules - Create your own Boundary rules. Know what to accept and what to reject in people's behaviors and opportunities for your life. Break your boundary rules and you're out.
11. Make your own Rules. Carve your own path in life. Shatter the stereotypes, glass ceilings, and molds. Forget what is expected and do what is necessary to live your life the right way for you to be happy, healthy, and wealthy.
12. Learn from your Mistakes. Have a growth mindset, see what went wrong, don't beat yourself up, learn and move on. As Edison said, I learned 1,000 ways not to make a light bulb. It only takes 1 right way to find your success - find. your success.

IT'S OK TO GIVE YOURSELF PERMISSION

1. Give yourself permission. You don't need anymore else's approval. You've got this.
2. Speak your mind respectfully from the heart. The real, no BS truth, sets you free.
3. Chase your dreams. Follow your own path. If the road less traveled makes your heart soar; it is the key to your happiness.
4. Show your real inner strength by giving kindness and compassion freely. Be the kindness and compassion you want to see in the world.
5. Be fully responsible for your own happiness. No one else is responsible for how you feel, think, or behave. You are strong enough to ask for help if you want or need it.
6. Enjoy your own company. If a relationship isn't right, like yourself enough to fly solo. It's ok to to like yourself. Self love really is a thing. Having morals and keeping them is a real thing. Having boundaries and keeping them is a true sign of self respect. It is the key to being your truest Queen and

King. Only Queens and Kings attract Queens and Kings to them, so know who you are and who you want by your side.

7. Dance to your own rhythm. Care less about what others are doing and more about what is best for you.
8. Seek those that lift you up. Don't buy into the drama Mama. Toxic people, narcissists, and negative people only bring stress; avoid that mess.
9. Know how to take a compliment. One of the humblest acts of self love we can do is to accept a compliment with a simple 'Thank you'. It's not conceited or arrogant. Stop being your own worst critic.
10. Practice Boundary Club Rules. Create your own Boundary rules. Know what to accept and what to reject in people's behaviors and opportunities for your life. Break your boundary rules and you're out.
11. Make your own Rules. Carve your own path in life. Shatter stereotypes, glass ceilings, and molds. Forget what is expected, do what is necessary. Live your life your way to be happy, healthy, and wealthy.

12. Learn from your Mistakes. Have your own growth mindset.

    See what went wrong. Don't beat yourself up. Learn. Move on. As Edison said: I learned 1,000 ways not to make a light bulb. It only takes 1 right way to find success - find your success.

WHEN YOU LOVE SOMEONE

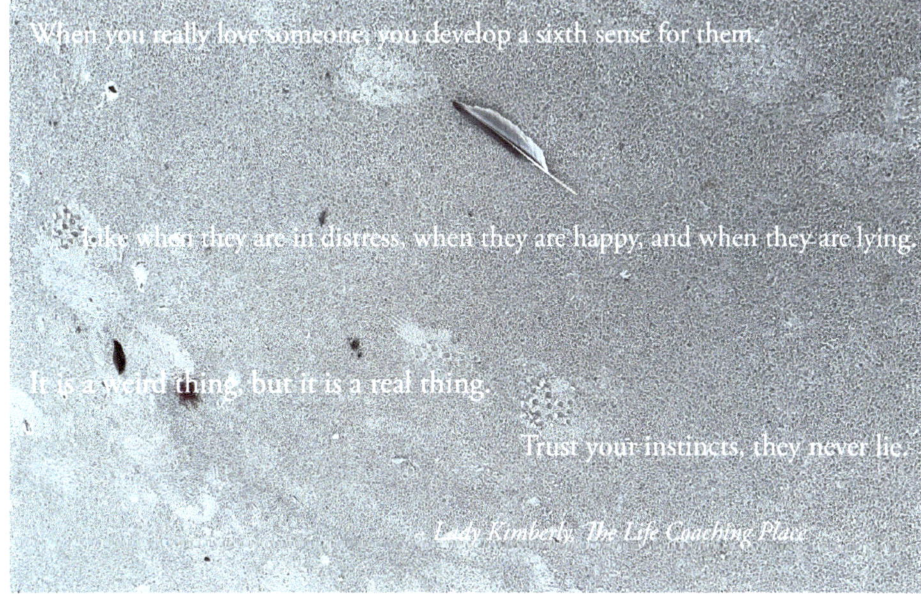
When you really love someone, you develop a sixth sense for them.
Like when they are in distress, when they are happy, and when they are lying.
It is a weird thing, but it is a real thing.
Trust your instincts, they never lie.
- Lady Kimberly, The Life Coaching Place

I LOVE YOU TO THE MOON & BACK

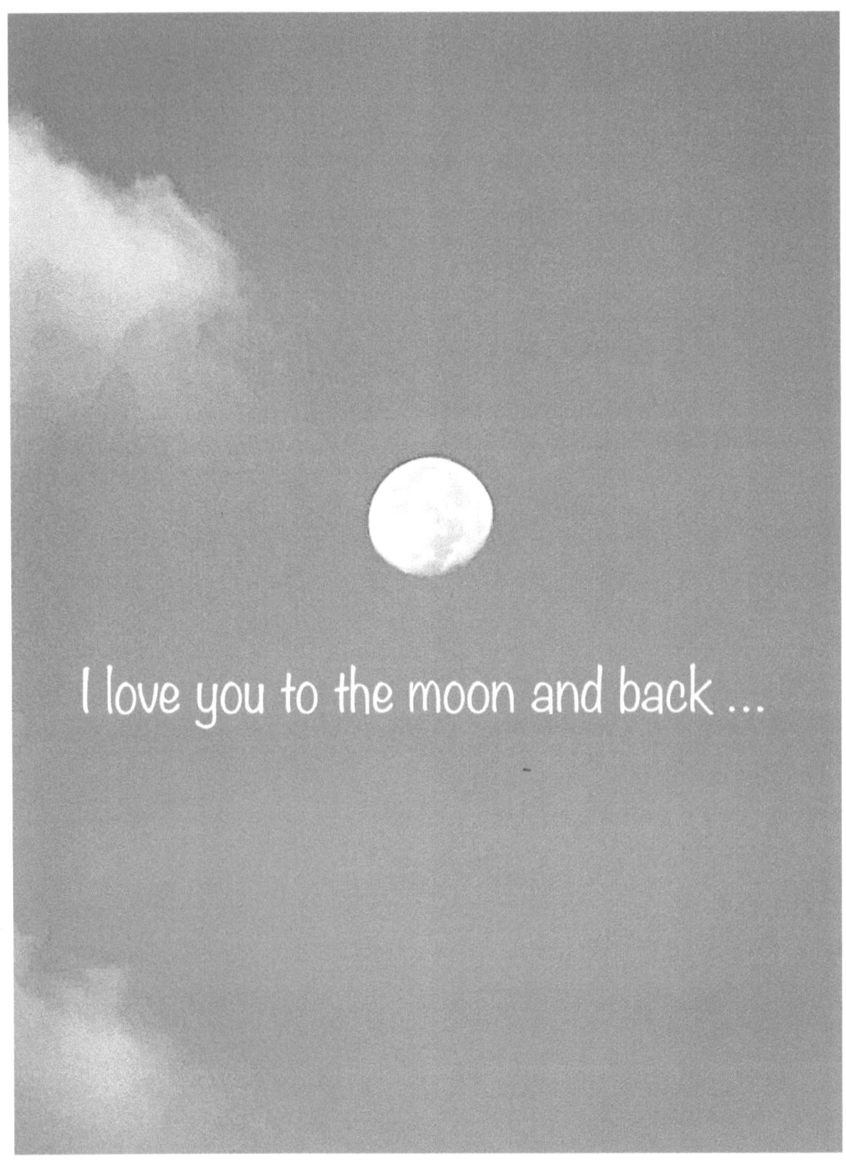
I love you to the moon and back ...

I LOVE YOU TO THE MOON & BACK 2

I love you to the moon & back . . .
~ Lady Kimberly

I LOVE YOU TO THE MOON & BACK 3

I love you to the moon & back …
~ Lady Kimberly

I LOVE YOU TO THE MOON & BACK 4

I love you to the moon & back …
~ Lady Kimberly

LET'S TAKE OUR HEARTS FOR A WALK BY THE SEA

Let's take our hearts
for a walk by the sea
and listen to the magical whispers
in the breeze ...
~ Lady Kimberly

WE LIVE EVERYDAY

Some say we only live once ...
But the truth is...
We only die once.
We live everyday.
So what are you doing
everyday to make it count?
~ Lady Kimberly

LOVE IS ABOUT

LOVE IS NOT FINDING
SOMEONE TO LIVE
WITH
IT'S FINDING SOMEONE
YOU CAN'T LIVE
WITHOUT.
~ Lady Kimberly

I AM THE MOON, TO SHINE IN YOUR DARKEST HOUR

Everyone else wanted to be the
sun to lighten up your days.
I am the moon, to shine in your
darkest hour and add magic to
your nights when you need me
the most.
- Lady Kimberly

DON'T WORRY IF YOU MAKE WAVES

Don't worry if you make waves simply
by being yourself.
The moon does it all the time.
It takes an incredibly brave woman to
live as she wishes - on her own terms,
free, wild and loving herself as she is.
- Lady Kimberly

HIS ACTIONS SHOW HOW HE FEELS ABOUT YOU

Regardless of what he says,
it is how he treats you
that shows how he feels about you.
Words are used to Manipulate.
Words keep you right where he wants you.
His actions show you what you really need to know.
~ Lady Kimberly

EVERYTHING BUILDS UPON TRUST

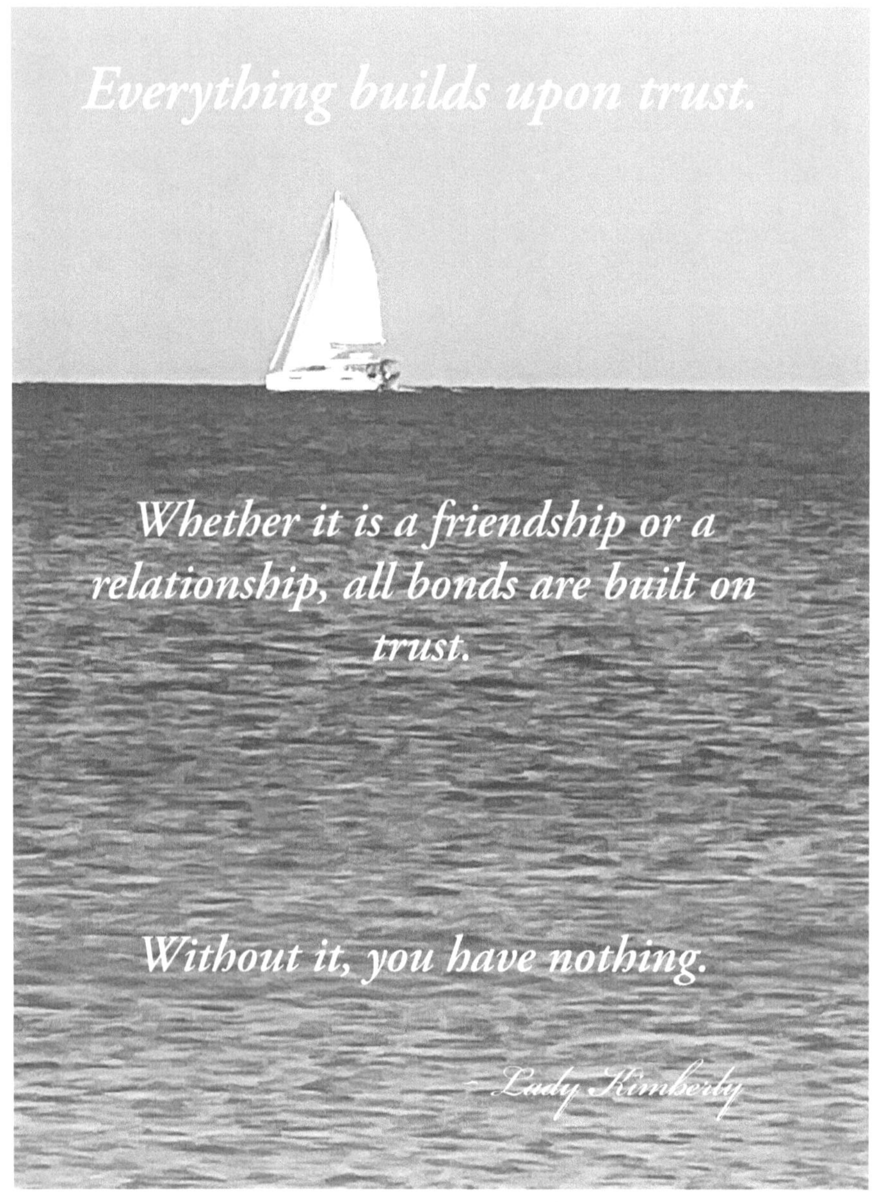
Everything builds upon trust.
Whether it is a friendship or a relationship, all bonds are built on trust.
Without it, you have nothing.
- Lady Kimberly

About the Author & Photographer

LADY KIMBERLY MOTES DOTY

Lady Kimberly, a retired technology specialist, who has now embarked on a new chapter in her life. As an Ordained Minister, Natural Health Specialist , and esteemed author, she has achieved bestseller status with her books in English, French, Spanish, and Italian. In search of inspiration, she can often be found on the picturesque beaches of Florida and the Carolina's.

Lady Kimberly's philosophy encapsulates her optimistic outlook on life:

"Everyday is your new day for a happily ever after. What are you doing today to make yours happen?"

A California girl nurtured in the heart of the Midwest, she always harbored a deep desire to reside in sunny Florida. Now, she is living her dream alongside her husband on the enchanting gulf coast.

Blessed with two daughters and four grandchildren, Lady Kimberly cherishes the joys of family. Moreover, she boasts an illustrious lineage as a direct descendant of the esteemed French Normandy de la Motte Family. Her ancestors played a pivotal role in assisting the Duke of Normandy, William the Conqueror, in ascending to the throne as the King of England. It is worth noting that both the former Queen of England and the current King of England trace their lineage back to William the Conqueror.

The legacy of the de la Motte family can still be experienced today, as their magnificent castles and chateaus dot the landscapes of Europe and the Middle East. Through her remarkable heritage and unwavering pursuit of her passions, Lady Kimberly exemplifies a life lived with passion, purpose and a commitment to embracing the extraordinary.

ADDITIONAL INFORMATION ABOUT LADY KIMBERLY

For additional information about Lady Kimberly or to send her a message, check out her Author Profile on Amazon:

https://www.amazon.com/author/ladykimberly

Look for more of Lady Kimberly's current and upcoming books:

A Children's Guide to a Godly Way of Life - Just Published

A Godly Way of Life - Published

Emma and Luna's Crazy Fat Tail Adventure - Coming Soon

Faith and Fear - Coming Soon

Heaven - Coming Soon

If the Alphabet Grew Out of The Sea - v2 Coming Soon

Life As Cake - Top 10 Best Selling New Release

Praying Specific For The Life God Intended For You - Coming Soon

Pregnancy, Nausea and Vomiting - Top 10 Best Selling New Release

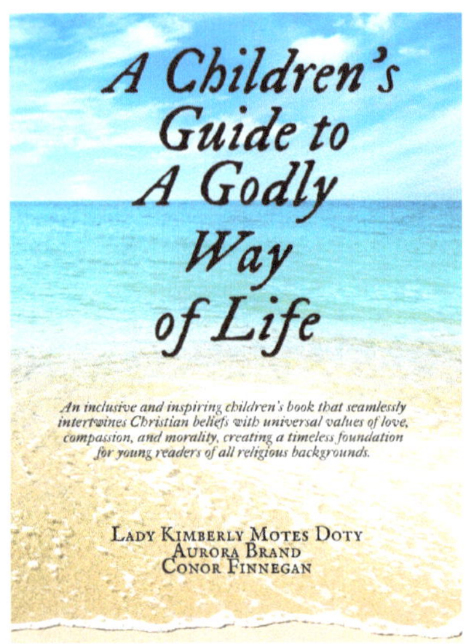
A Children's Guide to A Godly Way of Life
An inclusive and inspiring children's book that seamlessly intertwines Christian beliefs with universal values of love, compassion, and morality, creating a timeless foundation for young readers of all religious backgrounds.
Lady Kimberly Motes Doty
Aurora Brand
Conor Finnegan

A Godly Way of Life
LADY KIMBERLY MOTES DOTY

LADY KIMBERLY MOTES DOTY

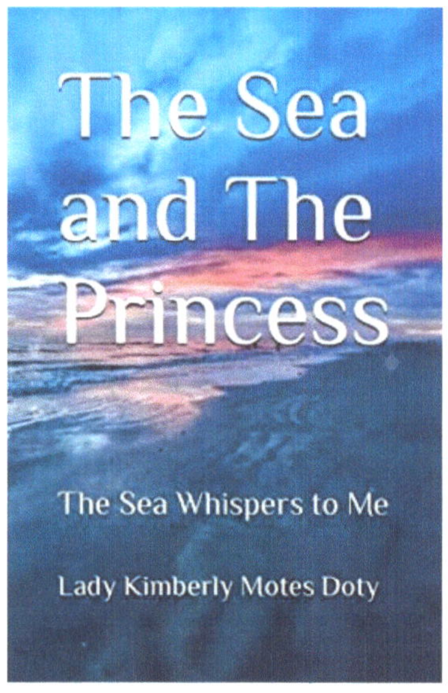
The Sea and The Princess
The Sea Whispers to Me
Lady Kimberly Motes Doty

Si El Alfabeto Creció Fuera De Mar (Spanish Edition) - v2 Coming Soon

Si l'Alphabet A Grandi Hors De La Mer (French Edition) - v2 Coming Soon

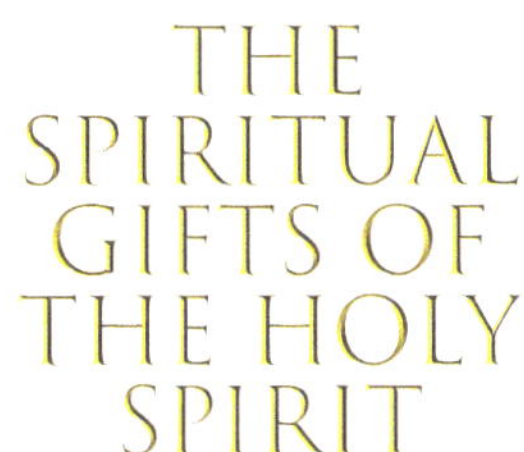
THE
SPIRITUAL
GIFTS OF
THE HOLY
SPIRIT

Spiritual Gifts of the Holy Spirit - Coming Soon

The Bellydance Pilates Walking Program - Top 10 Best Selling New Release

The Mermaid and The Pillar - Coming Soon

The Sea and The Princess: The Sea Whispers To Me - Top 20 Best Selling New Release

The Wounds The Won't Heal - Coming Soon

Your New Day Dawning - #1 Best Selling New Release

If The Alphabet Grew Out of The Sea
Lady KimberlyMotes Doty

Si El Alfabeto Creció Fuera De Mar
Lady Kimberly Motes Doty

Si l'Alphabet A Grandi Hors De La Mer
Lady KimberlyMotes Doty

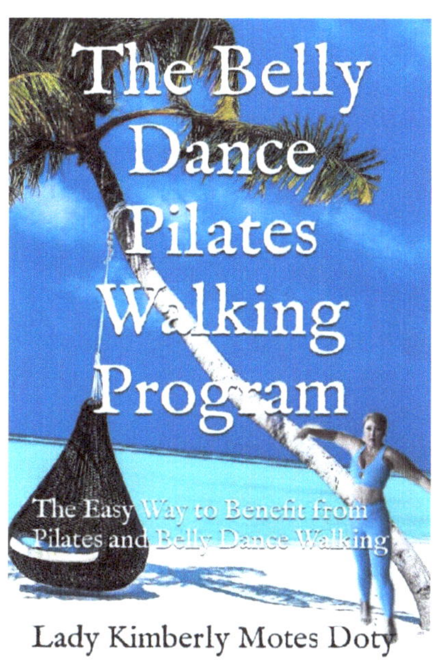
The Belly Dance Pilates Walking Program
The Easy Way to Benefit from Pilates and Belly Dance Walking
Lady Kimberly Motes Doty

Les Programmes De Marche Pilates Danse Du Ventre
Le Moyen Facile De Profiter Du Pilates Et De La Danse Du Ventre
Lady Kimberly Motes Doty

LADY KIMBERLY MOTES DOTY
Life As Cake
Learning to Manage Life so Life Doesn't Manage You

To upgrade your home, business or church with the inspirationals, quotes, sayings or photographs from Lady Kimberly's inspirational prayer walks, you can create your unique style. Choose your favorite Bible verse or your favorite photograph. Whatever you choose, it will be beautiful!

https://www.artpal.com/LadyKimberly

Everyday
is YOUR
day for
YOUR
happily
ever after.
Be with someone who
chooses you everyday
not just when they are in
the mood for you.
Lady Kimberly

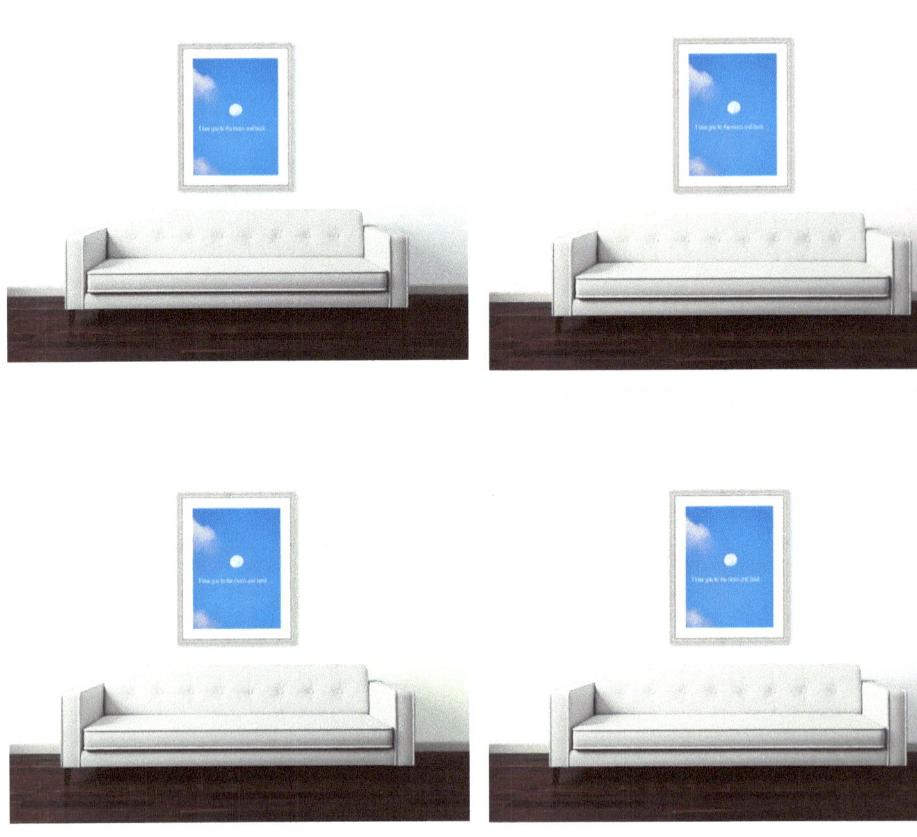

Whatever your style or aesthetic, you can can find it in Lady Kimberly's extensive art collections.

Choose one or a gallery wall

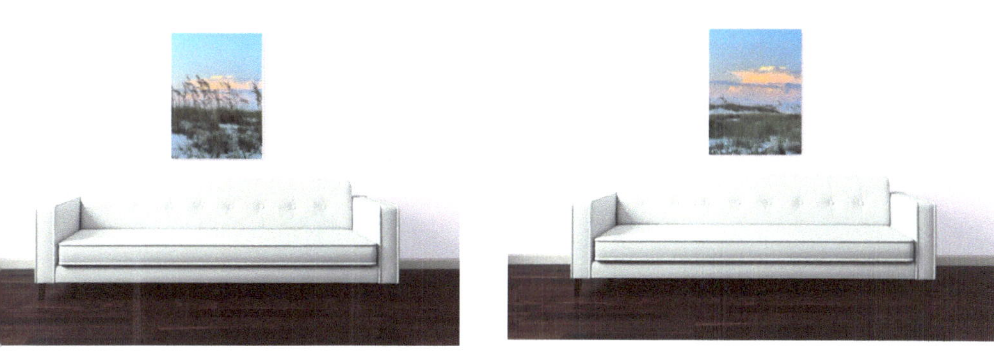

Maybe you just want to make it easier for your children remember the commandments from the Bible.

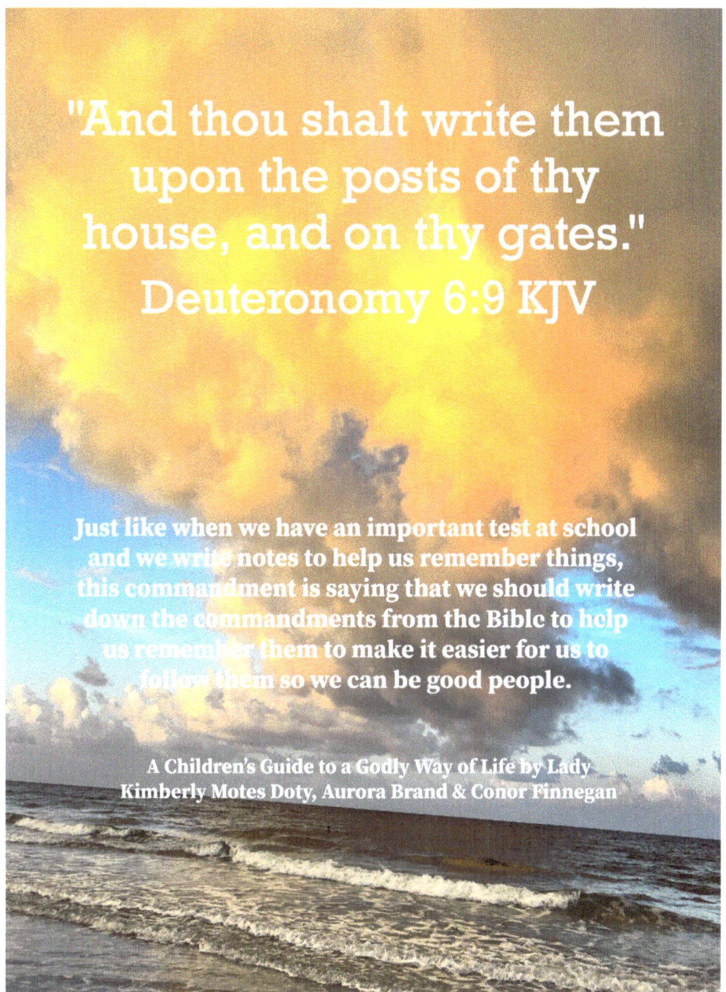
"And thou shalt write them upon the posts of thy house, and on thy gates."
Deuteronomy 6:9 KJV
Just like when we have an important test at school and we write notes to help us remember things, this commandment is saying that we should write down the commandments from the Bible to help us remember them to make it easier for us to follow them so we can be good people.
A Children's Guide to a Godly Way of Life by Lady Kimberly Motes Doty, Aurora Brand & Conor Finnegan

www.ingramcontent.com/pod-product-compliance
Lightning Source LLC
Chambersburg PA
CBHW061029100726
47911CB00001B/21

* 9 7 8 1 0 8 8 2 4 8 5 8 4 *